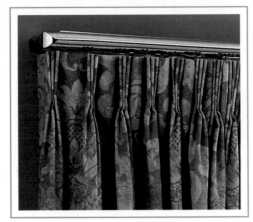

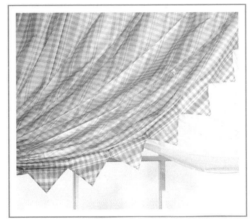

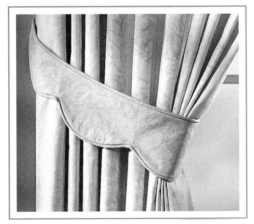

DECORATING WITH CURTAINS

DRESS UP YOUR WINDOWS WITH FRESH, FASHIONABLE CURTAINS

WINDOW CURTAINS OFFER ENDLESS DESIGN POSSIBILITIES FOR YOUR HOME.

WITH THE DRAPABLE, TEXTURAL QUALITIES OF FABRIC, THEY SOFTEN THE HARD,

FLAT SURFACES OF WOODWORK AND GLASS. THEY CAN PROVIDE PRIVACY AND

CONTROL DAYLIGHT OR SIMPLY ENHANCE A PRETTY VIEW. WITH CAREFULLY

SELECTED COLOR, STYLE, AND HARDWARE, CURTAINS CAN CAPTURE THE

ATTENTION IN A ROOM OR GRACIOUSLY BLEND WITH THE WALLS TO

SET THE STAGE FOR YOUR FURNITURE AND ARTWORK.

ABOVE ALL, YOUR CURTAINS ESTABLISH A MOOD AND

REFLECT YOUR PERSONAL DECORATING TASTE.

FORM & FUNCTION

Curtains soften the window's hard surfaces of wood and glass and bring more color and texture into the room. The process of selecting a curtain style, with the appropriate fabric and hardware, is easier once you have made two basic decisions. First, decide what functions you want the treatment to perform. Perhaps you need a treatment that blocks or limits light and provides privacy. You will want to select a lined treatment that can be opened and closed with ease, such as pleated draperies on a traverse rod. If privacy is not an issue, maybe you simply want to filter the light that enters the room with lightweight sheer curtains in either a traversing or stationary style. If the curtains are intended to be purely decorative, styles like tab curtains or rod-pocket curtains, which remain stationary, are appropriate. Curtains, by their design, can also change the visual size of the window. For instance, side curtain panels that extend out onto the wall visually widen the window. If those

Stationary rod-pocket curtains (page 49) are parted and tucked behind holdbacks, revealing light-filtering sheer curtains mounted on a separate rod behind them.

CURTAINS

CURTAINS

Created by: The Editors of Cowles Creative Publishing, Inc.

Library of Congress Cataloging-in-Publication Data
Curtains / the Home Decorating Institute.
    p. cm. -- (Creative textiles)
  ISBN 0-86573-412-7 (softcover)
  1. Drapery. 2. Sewing. 3. Drapery in interior decoration. I. Home Decorating
Institute (Minnetonka, Minn.) II. Cowles Creative Publishing. III. Series.
TT390.C88 1997
646.2'1--dc21   97-29097

THE HOME DECORATING INSTITUTE®

COWLES
Creative Publishing, Inc.

CONTENTS

same curtain panels are hung within the window frame, over the glass, they make the window appear narrower.

Second, determine what mood or personality you want the window treatment to convey. Contemporary taste favors sleek-lined, no-frills treatments and hardware that emphasizes function over form. Textured tab curtains or banded curtains on wrought-iron rods could express this taste. Lovers of tradition may prefer the timeless look of pleated draperies on ornate rods or rich gathered rod-pocket treatments done in elegant fabrics. Ruffles and fullness are romantic and feminine in large flowery prints, while small prints and nubby textures exude homespun charm. If your room plan is eclectic, you may want to use the curtain style to establish a common theme among the elements or simply to blend with the walls, providing a quiet backdrop for showcasing unique furniture and artwork.

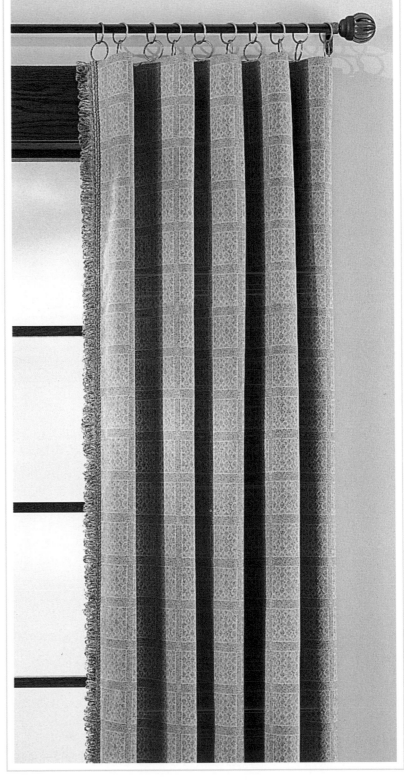

Simple curtain panels (page 81), hung from rings on a sleek rod, provide an understated, yet sophisticated, treatment that would blend well in many decorating schemes.

DESIGN ELEMENTS
Color

COLORFUL INFLUENCES

No other design element has as much impact on the decorating plan of a home as color. Through the effective use of color, we can alter visual perceptions of space and size, influence the energy level and moods of the people in the room, and even adjust the perceived room temperature. Blues, greens, and aquas, the cool colors, have a calming effect, while reds, oranges, and yellows bring warmth and excitement. Pastels expand space, while bold, dramatic, and dark colors make a room seem smaller. The intensity of these different color influences depends on the amount of decorating surface devoted to them. Window treatments often represent a large proportion of that decorating surface, especially in rooms with several windows, large windows, or floor-length treatments. With so much potential for design influence, it is important to select curtain colors carefully.

Whether you are adding new curtains to an existing color scheme or are decorating the entire room at once, because of its relative size, the window treatment will become a dominant force in that scheme. The color value used may determine whether the curtain becomes a focal point or blends into the background. If it is your intention to showcase furniture, artwork, or an Oriental rug, for instance, make curtains of the same color value and hue as the walls surrounding them so that they become a stylish backdrop. Make curtains that contrast in color value or hue from the walls, if you want the window to become a focal point in the room.

Here are some other color tricks you can play with your curtains:

Soften a strong monochromatic color scheme by accenting the curtains with decorative trim or narrow banding in a complementary color.

Add drama to a neutral color scheme with jewel-tone tie-tabs on a soft, subtle curtain.

Coordinate several mismatched elements in an eclectic room with an all-over print curtain fabric that combines all their colors.

Make an attached valance in a darker hue than the curtain to visually lower the height of the window, or in a lighter hue to visually raise the height of the window.

When making white sheer curtains, select a blue-white to give the room a cool, serene aura; select a creamy white to suggest warmth and coziness.

Pleated draperies sewn in a print with the same color value as the wall develop a passive, yet stylish, backdrop for showcasing furniture and accessories.

High contrast between the bold wall color and the white curtains ensures that all eyes will be drawn to this picturesque look.

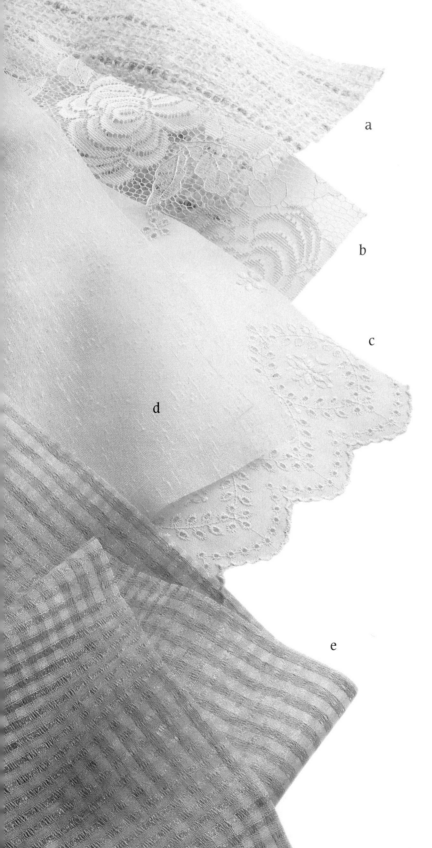

a

b

c

d

e

Decorator fabrics suitable for curtains have characteristics not found in fashion fabrics. Thread counts, meaning the number of threads per square inch (centimeter), are generally higher in decorator fabrics, making them stronger. Stain-resistant finishes are usually applied to decorator fabrics, since they must go for long periods of time without being cleaned. When cleaning is necessary, most decorator fabrics must be dry-cleaned to avoid shrinkage.

The weave pattern, fiber content, and weight of the fabric selected for your curtains will have an impact on their finished appearance, their durability, and their ability to control light. Lightweight open weaves can be used whenever you want curtains that let in light. These include casements (a), laces (b), eyelets (c), and sheers (d). Often these fabrics are woven in 118" (300 cm) widths, with the width intended to run vertically, allowing you to make floor-length sheer curtains without seams. Novelty sheers (e) have interesting textural features, sometimes arranged in stripes. Most sheers are made of polyester for strength and stability, though they may also contain other decorative fibers. Natural fibers, including cotton and linen, are also used for sheer and lightweight fabrics.

Mediumweight fabrics include a wide range of fiber contents and weave structures. Plain weaves (f) may be solid in color or printed and include chintz, which has a surface glaze. Satin weaves

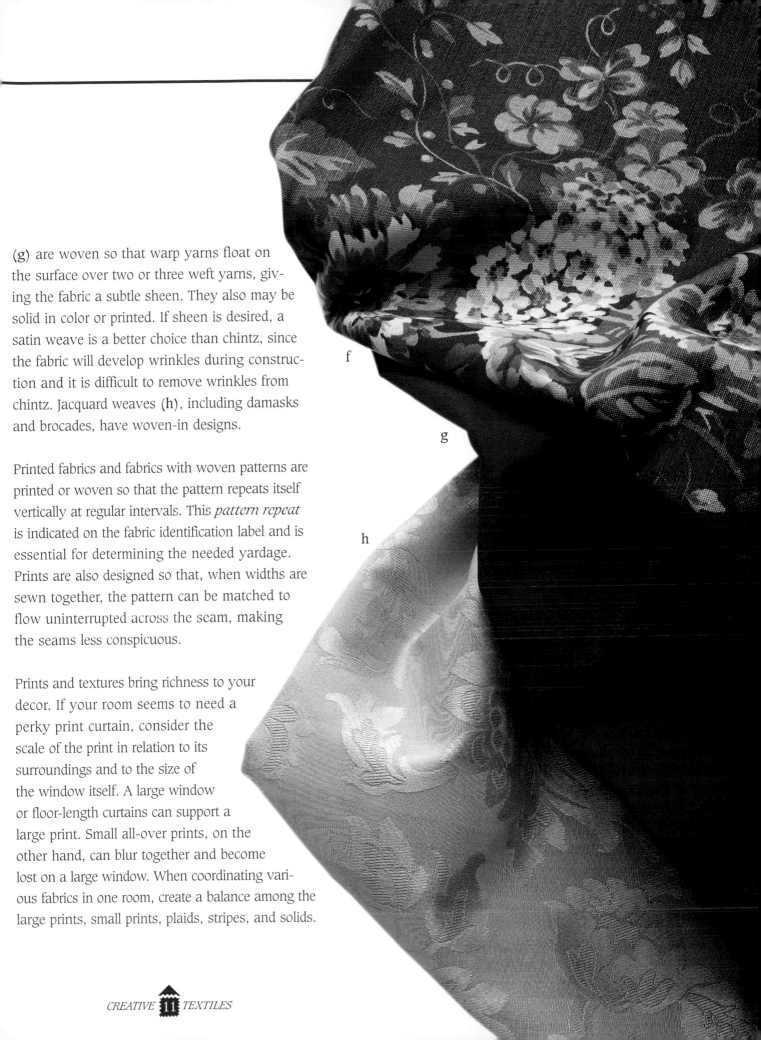

(g) are woven so that warp yarns float on the surface over two or three weft yarns, giving the fabric a subtle sheen. They also may be solid in color or printed. If sheen is desired, a satin weave is a better choice than chintz, since the fabric will develop wrinkles during construction and it is difficult to remove wrinkles from chintz. Jacquard weaves (h), including damasks and brocades, have woven-in designs.

Printed fabrics and fabrics with woven patterns are printed or woven so that the pattern repeats itself vertically at regular intervals. This *pattern repeat* is indicated on the fabric identification label and is essential for determining the needed yardage. Prints are also designed so that, when widths are sewn together, the pattern can be matched to flow uninterrupted across the seam, making the seams less conspicuous.

Prints and textures bring richness to your decor. If your room seems to need a perky print curtain, consider the scale of the print in relation to its surroundings and to the size of the window itself. A large window or floor-length curtains can support a large print. Small all-over prints, on the other hand, can blur together and become lost on a large window. When coordinating various fabrics in one room, create a balance among the large prints, small prints, plaids, stripes, and solids.

*B*ASICS

CLASSIC & TIMELESS

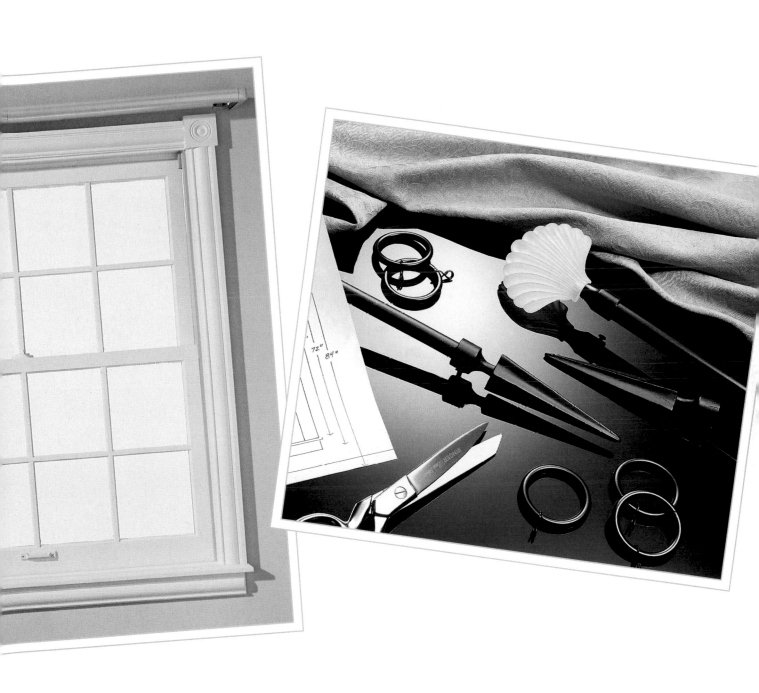

STYLISH & TRENDY

Hardware NEEDS

The hardware you select can be decorative as well as functional. For elaborate window treatments, traditional poles with detailed finials are available, as well as decorative tieback holders. And sleek, contemporary hardware is available for a more understated look. For a creative, nontraditional look, consider using decorative knobs (page 73) or other items as hardware.

Select the type of hardware you want before measuring for a window treatment. The cut length of drapery panels will vary, depending on the hardware used.

TRAVERSE DRAPERY RODS

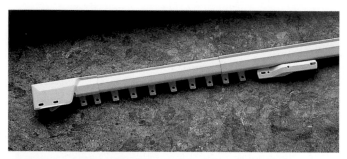

Conventional traverse rods are available in white, ivory, and wood tones.

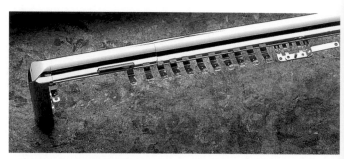

Contemporary traverse rods have metallic and pearlized finishes in several colors.

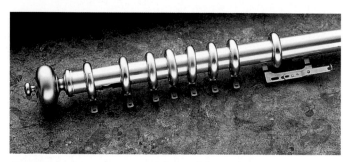

Brass traverse pole sets, with or without rings, come with various finial styles. The poles are plain or fluted.

Wood traverse pole sets with rings are available in several finishes.

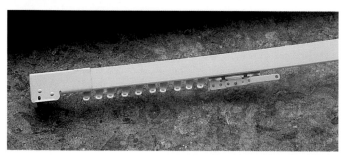

Flexible traverse rods are used for pleated draperies on bay windows. A single flexible rod is easily installed into a bay opening.

Marbleized traverse pole sets, available in white or black, have a sculptured, classic look.

CURTAIN RODS

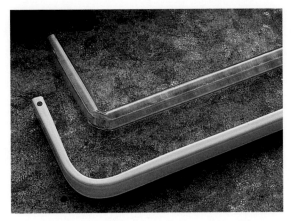

Narrow curtain rods are used for rod-pocket window treatments. When sheer fabric is used, select a rod of clear or translucent plastic that will not show through the fabric.

Tension rods, used inside window frames for cafe curtains, are held in place by the pressure of a spring inside the rod. Because mounting brackets are not used, the woodwork is not damaged by screws.

Cafe rods are used with or without rings. Available in several finishes, including brass and enamel, they are used for hand-drawn window treatments or tie-tab curtains.

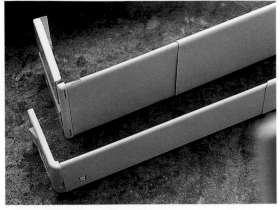

Wide curtain rods are available in both 2¹/2" (6.5 cm) and 4¹/2" (11.5 cm) widths. They add depth and interest to rod-pocket window treatments. Corner connectors make these rods suitable for bay and corner windows.

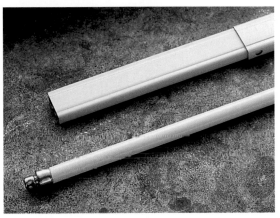

Sash rods use shallow mounting brackets so the window treatment hangs close to the glass. Available flat or round, they are commonly used for stretched curtains on doors.

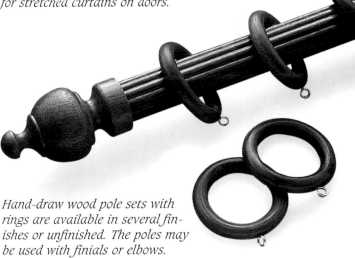

Hand-draw wood pole sets with rings are available in several finishes or unfinished. The poles may be used with finials or elbows.

HARDWARE ACCESSORIES

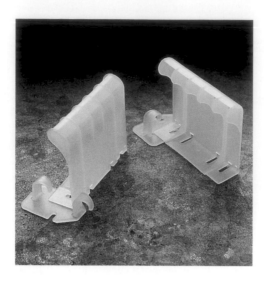

Concealed tieback holders fit behind the last fold of pleated or rod-pocket draperies to prevent the tieback from crushing the draperies. The projection is adjustable.

Decorative tieback holders are used with fabric or cord tiebacks to hold draperies in place.

Installing HARDWARE

Support drapery rods with center brackets to prevent them from bowing. The brackets are usually positioned at intervals of 45" (115 cm) or less, across the width of the rod. Whenever possible, screw the brackets into wall studs. If it is necessary to position brackets between wall studs into drywall or plaster, use molly bolts for installing hardware that will support heavy window treatments. For supporting lightweight window treatments or for installing tieback holders, plastic anchors may be used instead of molly bolts.

HOW TO INSTALL *H*ARDWARE USING MOLLY BOLTS

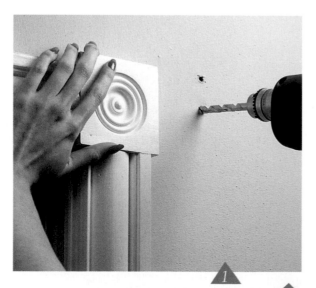

1 . . . . . . Mark screw locations on wall. Drill holes for molly bolts into drywall or plaster; drill-bit diameter depends on size of molly bolt.

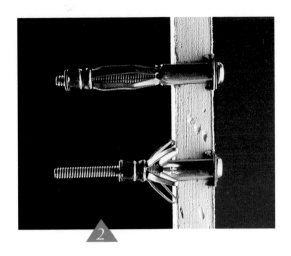

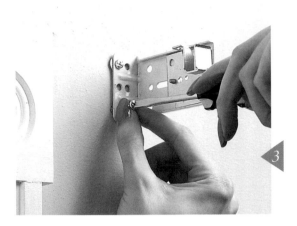

2 . . . . . . Tap molly bolt into drilled hole, using hammer. Tighten screw; molly bolt expands, preventing it from pulling out of the wall.

3 . . . . . . Remove screw from molly bolt; insert screw into hole in hardware and into installed molly bolt. Screw the hardware securely in place.

HOW TO INSTALL *H*ARDWARE USING PLASTIC ANCHORS

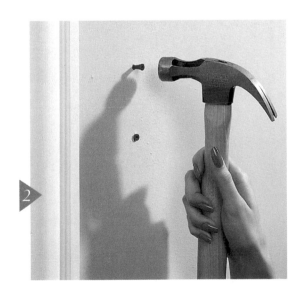

1 . . . . . . Hold hardware at desired location; for tieback holders, position tieback holder below end bracket of drapery rod so drapery will hang straight at sides. Mark screw locations.

2 . . . . . . Drill holes for plastic anchors into drywall or plaster. Tap plastic anchors into drilled holes, using hammer.

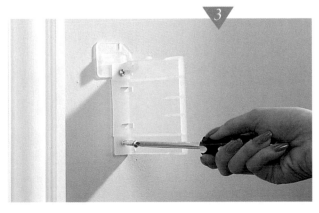

3 . . . . . . Insert screw into hardware and into installed plastic anchor. Screw hardware securely in place; the anchor expands in drywall, preventing it from pulling out of the wall.

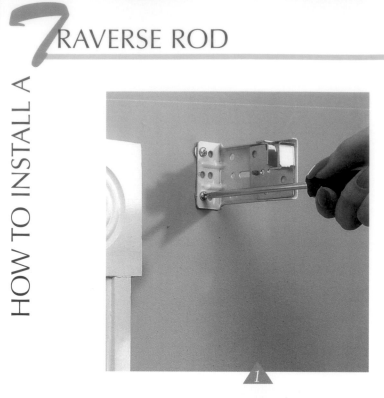

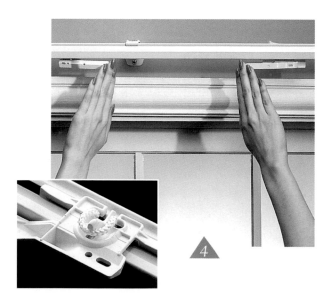

1 . . . . . . Mount the end rod brackets with U-shaped socket facing upward.

2 . . . . . . Hook lipped support clip of center bracket over center of rod; position rod, fitting ends of rod into end brackets. Mark screw holes for center bracket.

3 . . . . . . Take rod down, and mount center bracket. Lift the rod into position again; snap center support clip over rod, hooking it into groove at front of rod. Using screwdriver, turn metal cam on underside of support clip counterclockwise, locking clip in place.

4 . . . . . . Push overlap and underlap master slides to opposite ends of rod. At left side, reach behind underlap slide for the cord. Pull cord slightly to form small loop; hook loop securely over plastic finger that projects from the back of master slide (inset).

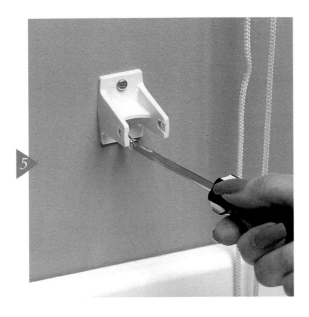

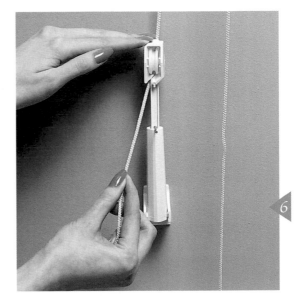

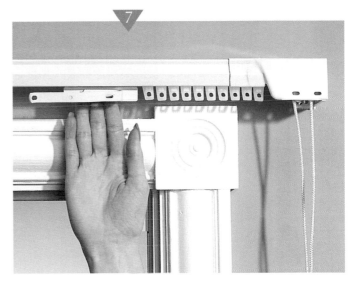

5 ...... Separate the stem from pulley base; hold base against wall near the floor, directly below a point 2" (5 cm) in from the right end bracket of rod. Mark screw locations; mount bracket.

6 ...... Attach stem to pulley base. Pull up on cord housing, exposing hole on inner stem. Insert small nail through hole so stem remains extended. Attach cord to pulley, slipping loop end of cord through slot in cord housing.

7 ...... Reach behind overlap master slide at right end of rod; locate two knots at back of slide.

8 ...... Pull the right-hand knot until cord hanging at side of rod is taut against pulley wheel. Tie a new knot in cord at back of slide, with excess cord hanging down. Remove nail from inner stem of pulley. Cut off excess cord; tighten knot securely.

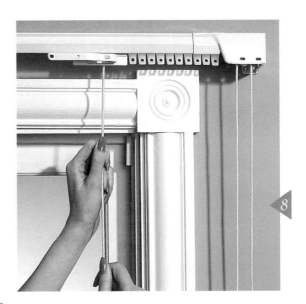

$\mathcal{I}$nstalling PVC POLES

PVC pipe can be used as a lightweight and inexpensive alternative to wood or metal decorator poles. PVC pipe is available in a variety of sizes, with inside diameters ranging from 1" to 4" (2.5 to 10 cm). PVC elbows, available in each size, can be used to make a pole with returns. Or, if desired, decorator finials can be attached to the ends of the PVC pole.

LIST *of* MATERIALS

FOR POLES WITH FINIALS
▸ PVC pipe in desired diameter; select size of pipe to fit end of finial.
▸ Two decorative finials.
▸ Keyhole support brackets, for ends and center supports; 1/2" (1.3 cm) hex-head screws.
▸ 1 1/2" (3.8 cm) hex-head screws, for installing brackets into wall studs; or molly bolts or plastic anchors, for installing into drywall or plaster.
▸ Scrap of wood.
▸ Sandpaper; hacksaw; drill and drill bits.

FOR POLES WITH ELBOW RETURNS
▸ PVC pipe in desired diameter.
▸ Two PVC elbows, preferably without collars, in size to match pipe.
▸ Keyhole support brackets, for center supports; 1/2" (1.3 cm) hex-head screws.
▸ Two 2" (5 cm) angle irons, for mounting at returns.
▸ 1 1/2" (3.8 cm) flat-head screws, for installing angle irons into wall studs; or molly bolts or plastic anchors, for installing into drywall or plaster.
▸ Two 10 × 1" (2.5 cm) round-head bolts.

HOW TO MAKE & INSTALL A PVC POLE WITH FINIALS

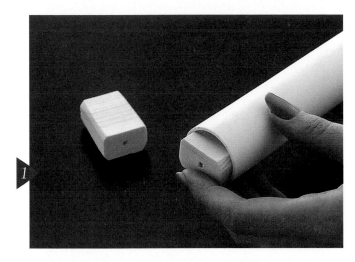

1...... Cut PVC pipe to the desired length, using a hacksaw; sand the ends. Cut a scrap of wood to wedge snugly into each end of the pipe. Drill a hole in center of each wood scrap, using a drill bit slightly smaller than the finial screw. Insert the wood scraps into ends of the pole.

2...... Attach finial to wood scrap. Repeat for the opposite end of the pole.

3...... Hold the pole to the wall at desired location; mark for placement of keyhole support brackets on wall, at least 1/2" (1.3 cm) from finials. If additional support bracket is needed, mark for placement near center. Install brackets, using 1 1/2" (3.8 cm) hex-head screws, into wall studs; if brackets are not positioned at the wall studs, use molly bolts or plastic anchors (page 16 or 17).

4...... Hold pole up to the brackets; mark placement for 1/2" (1.3 cm) screws on back of the pole. Predrill holes for screws; insert screws into the holes, leaving heads of screws standing slightly away from back of the pole. Mount pole, inserting the screw heads into the keyholes.

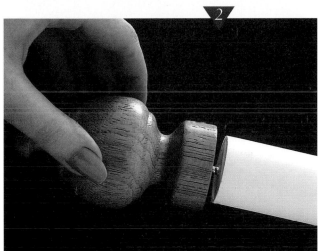

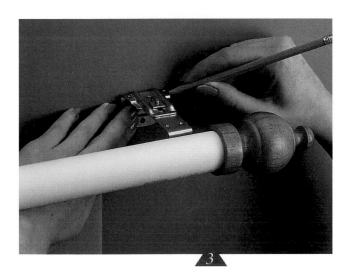

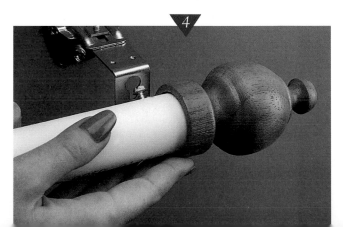

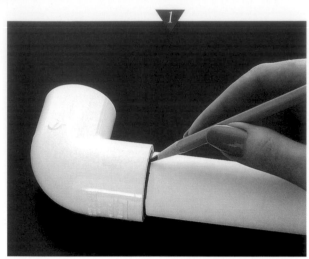

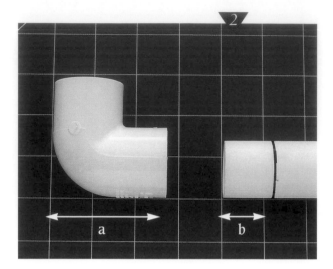

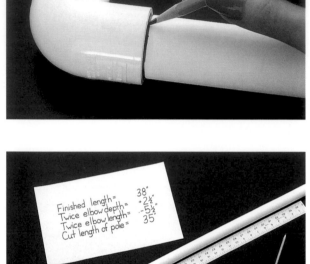

1 ..... Slide elbow onto the pipe as far as possible; mark the depth of elbow on the pipe.

2 ..... Remove elbow; measure the elbow length (a) from the outer edge of one side to the opening on the opposite side. Then measure the elbow depth (b) from end of pipe to the mark.

3 ..... Cut the PVC pipe, using a hacksaw, with length equal to the desired finished length of the pole plus twice the elbow depth minus twice the elbow length. Sand the cut ends.

4 ..... Slide the elbow onto a small remaining piece of PVC pipe as far as possible. Measure from the outer edge of elbow to the desired return depth on pipe; mark.

5 ..... Remove the pipe from the elbow. Cut the pipe with a hacksaw; cut a second piece the same length for the opposite return. Sand the cut ends.

6 ..... Lay angle iron over end of return pipe; mark pipe with location of hole closest to the back of angle iron. Drill hole through marked side of the pipe, using a 1/4" drill bit. Repeat for the second return pipe.

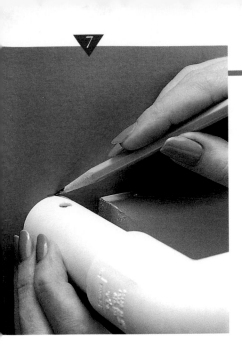

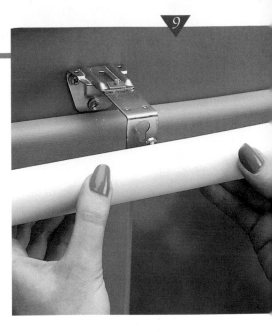

7...... Assemble PVC pole, sliding pipe pieces into the elbows as far as possible, with holes in return pieces centered on top. Hold pole to wall in the desired location; mark wall at top center of return piece.

8...... Mount angle irons on wall, with tops of angle irons centered at the marks, using 1½" (3.8 cm) flathead screws into wall studs; if angle irons are not positioned at wall studs, use molly bolts or plastic anchors (pages 16 and 17). Mount pole over angle irons, aligning holes in pipe to holes in angle irons; insert 10 × 1" (2.5 cm) round-head bolts through holes to secure.

9...... Mark the wall for center keyhole support bracket, if needed; mark placement for screw on back of pole. Remove pole; install bracket on wall, and insert screw into back of pole, as on page 21, step 4. Remount pole.

HOW TO HANG *R*OD-POCKET CURTAINS ON A PVC POLE

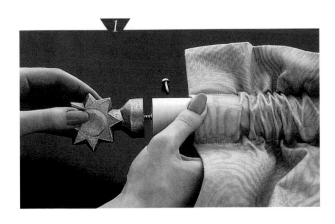

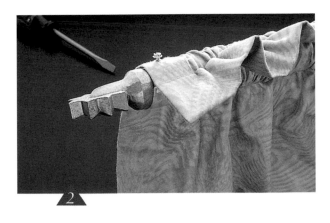

1...... Remove pole from wall; remove screws, if any, from the back of pole. Remove elbows or finials. Insert the pole into rod pocket of the curtain; reattach finials or elbows. Distribute fullness evenly.

2...... Locate screw holes, if any, and insert screws through curtain fabric. Remount the pole on the brackets or angle irons.

$\mathcal{M}$easuring THE WINDOW

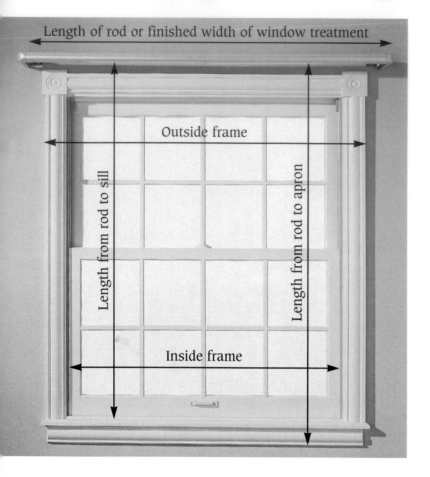

Length of rod or finished width of window treatment

Outside frame

Length from rod to sill

Length from rod to apron

Inside frame

TIPS FOR MEASURING

Allow ½" (1.3 cm) clearance between the bottom of the drapery and the floor when measuring for floor-length draperies. For loosely woven fabrics, allow 1" (2.5 cm) clearance.

Allow 4" to 6" (10 to 15 cm) clearance above baseboard heaters for safety.

Measure for all draperies in the room to the same height from the floor for a uniform look. Use the highest window in the room as the standard for measuring for the treatments on the other windows.

Make underdraperies ½" (1.3 cm) shorter than the overdraperies at the top and bottom, so they will not show above or below the overdraperies.

After selecting the window treatment, install the hardware and take the necessary measurements. For accurate measurements, use a folding ruler or metal tape measure. Measure and record the measurements for each window separately, even if the windows appear to be the same size.

Depending on the style of the window treatment, rods and mounting boards may be mounted inside or outside the window frame. For an inside mount, install the hardware inside the top of the frame so the molding is exposed. For an outside mount, install the hardware at the top of the window frame or on the wall above the window. When the hardware is mounted above the window frame, visual height is added to the window.

Some window treatments can be mounted so they cover part of the wall at the sides of the window, adding visual width. When window treatments are mounted onto the wall, more glass can be exposed, letting in more light.

You will need to determine the finished length and finished width of the window treatment. Then determine the cut

length and cut width by adding the amounts needed for hems, rod pockets, seams, and fullness. If a patterned fabric is used, you will also need to allow extra fabric for matching the pattern (page 26).

To determine the finished length of the window treatment, measure from the rod or the mounting board to where you want the lower edge of the window treatment. The measurement is usually taken from the top of the rod or board. When decorative rods are used, the measurement is taken from the pin hole in one of the rings or slides. Depending on the style of the treatment, you may need to add to this measurement an amount for heading or clearance above the rod. Specific instructions for determining the finished length are included in the cutting directions for each window treatment in this book.

To determine the finished width of the window treatment, measure the length of the drapery rod or mounting board. For some treatments, it may also be necessary to measure the width of the return (opposite).

Overlap is the area where the drapery panels lap over each other at the center of a two-way traverse rod. The standard overlap is 3½" (9 cm).

Stacking space is the distance from the sides of the window to the brackets, that allows draperies on traverse rods to clear, or partially clear, the window when the draperies are drawn open; this is sometimes referred to as *stackback*. Stationary window treatments may also be mounted so they "stack" at the sides of the window.

Projection is the distance the rod or mounting board stands out from the wall.

Return is the portion of the drapery extending from the corner of the rod to the wall, enclosing the brackets of the drapery hardware. For draperies mounted on traverse rods, the return is ½" (1.3 cm) more than the projection of the rod.

Fullness of window treatments can vary, depending on the look desired. It is referred to as two, two-and-one-half, or three times fullness; for example, two times fullness means that the width of the window treatment measures two times the length of the rod or mounting board. For mediumweight to heavyweight fabrics, use two to two-and-one-half times fullness (left). For sheer and lightweight fabrics, use two-and-one-half to three times fullness (right).

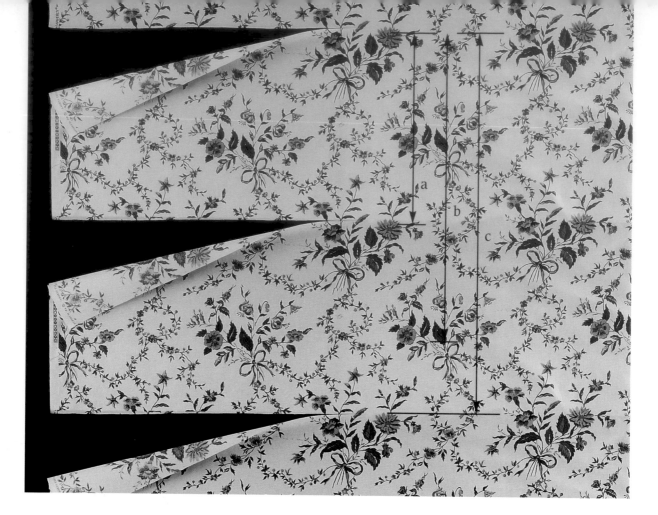

Cutting & Matching
PATTERNED FABRICS

For professional results, always match the pattern of a fabric at the seamlines. Extra yardage is usually needed in order to match the pattern.

The pattern repeat (a) is the lengthwise distance from one distinctive point on the pattern, such as the tip of a particular petal in a floral pattern, to the same point in the next pattern design. Some patterned fabrics have pattern repeat markings (+) printed on the selvage. These markings mark the beginning of each pattern repeat, and they are especially helpful for fabrics that include several similar designs.

Add the amounts needed for any hems, rod pockets, headings, ease, seam allowances, and fullness to the finished length, to determine how long the lengths of fabric need to be (b). Then round this measurement up to the next number divisible by the size of the pattern repeat. This is the cut length (c). For example, if the pattern repeat (a) is 19" (48.5 cm), and the finished length plus hems, rod pockets, and other allowances (b) is 30" (76 cm), the actual cut length (c) is 38" (96.5 cm). To have patterns match from one panel to the next, each panel must be cut at the same point on the pattern repeat.

To calculate the amount of fabric you will need, multiply the cut length by the number of fabric widths required for the project; add one additional pattern repeat so you can adjust the placement of the pattern on the cut lengths. This is the total fabric length in inches (centimeters); divide this measurement by 36" (100 cm) to determine the number of yards (meters) required.

TYPES OF SEAMS

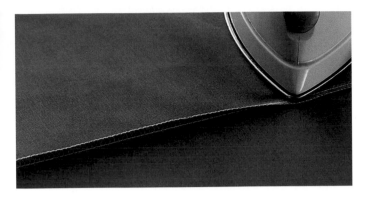

4-thread or 5-thread overlock seam, stitched on a serger, is self-finished and does not stretch out of shape. Press the seam allowances to one side.

Combination seams are stitched using the straight stitch on the conventional machine. The seam allowances are trimmed to ¼" (6 mm), trimming away the selvages, and finished using the zig-zag stitch (a) on a conventional machine or a 3-thread (b) or 2-thread (c) overlock stitch on a serger. Press the seam allowances to one side.

Straight-stitch seam, sewn on the conventional sewing machine, is pressed open for a smooth, flat seam. The selvages are trimmed away either before or after seaming the fabric. For lined window treatments, it is not necessary to finish the seam allowances.

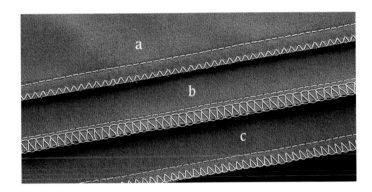

MATCHING A PATTERNED FABRIC

1   Position fabric widths right sides together, matching the selvages. Fold back the upper selvage until pattern matches; lightly press foldline.

2   Unfold selvage, and pin fabric widths together on foldline. Check the match from right side.

3   Repin fabric so pins are perpendicular to foldline; stitch on foldline, using straight stitch. Trim fabric to finished length plus hems, rod pockets, and other allowances, as calculated opposite.

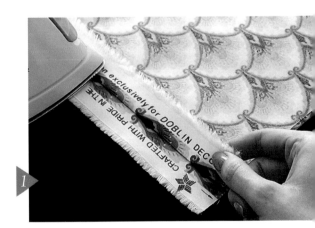

CURTAINS & DRAPERIES

FORMAL & CASUAL

SPLASHY & SUBDUED

Pleated DRAPERIES

Pleated draperies are a classic, ever-popular window treatment. Installed on traverse rods, they let in light when opened and offer privacy when closed. The pleats provide fullness to the draperies in uniform, graceful folds. The styling of pleated draperies can be varied by changing the pleat style and the pleat spacing (pages 40 and 41).

The instructions that follow are for a pair of drapery panels mounted on a two-way-draw traverse rod. When mounting the drapery rod, allow for the stacking space (page 25) at the sides of the window so the draperies will clear the window when they are open. The actual stacking space varies, depending on the weight of the fabric, the fullness of the draperies, and whether or not they are lined, but is estimated at one-third the width of the windows; allow for one-half of the stacking space on each side of the window.

If the draperies will hang from a conventional traverse rod, determine the finished length by measuring from the top of the rod to where you want the lower edge of the draperies; then add ½" (1.3 cm) so the draperies will extend above the rod. If the draperies will hang from a decorative rod, measure from the bottom of the rod to the desired finished length. If the draperies will hang from a pole set with rings, measure from the pin holes in the rings to the desired finished length.

Two-and-one-half times fullness is used for most draperies, but for sheers, three times fullness may be used. For lace draperies, use two-and-one-half times fullness so the pattern of the lace is noticeable in the finished draperies.

After the drapery panels are seamed and hemmed, use the Pleats Worksheet to determine the number and size of the pleats and the spaces between them.

DRAPERY WORKSHEETS

DRAPERY FABRIC WORKSHEET

Drapery Length	in. (cm)
Desired finished length (as determined on page 31)	
8" (20.5 cm) for heading	+
8" (20.5 cm) for 4" (10 cm) double-fold lower hem	+
Cut drapery length	=
Drapery Width	
Rod width (from end bracket to end bracket on conventional rods; from end ring to end ring on decorative rods)	
Allowance for two returns [projection of rod plus ½" (1.3 cm) for each return]	+
3½" (9 cm) for overlap	+
Finished drapery width	=
Total Number of Drapery Fabric Widths	
Finished drapery width multiplied by 2½ to 3 times for fullness	
Divided by width of fabric	÷
Total number of fabric widths needed, rounded up or down to nearest full width	=
Number of Drapery Fabric Widths per Panel	
Total number of fabric widths	
Divided by 2	÷
Number of fabric widths per panel	=

LINING FABRIC WORKSHEET

Lining Length	in. (cm)
Finished drapery length	
4" (10 cm) for 2" (5 cm) double-fold lower hem	+
Cut lining length	=
Number of Lining Widths	
Calculate as for Total Number of Drapery Fabric Widths (above).	

PLEATS WORKSHEET

After completing step 3 (opposite), use this worksheet to determine the number and size of pleats and the spaces between them. The recommended amount of fabric required for each pleat is 4" to 6" (10 to 15 cm). The recommended space between pleats is 3½" to 4" (9 to 10 cm). If the calculation from the worksheets results in pleats or spaces that are greater than the amount recommended, add one more pleat and space. If the calculation results in pleats or spaces smaller than the amount recommended, subtract one pleat and space.

Finished Panel Width	in. (cm)
Finished drapery width (figured left)	
Divided by 2	÷
Finished panel width	=
Number of Pleats per Panel	
Number of drapery fabric widths per panel (figured left)	
Multiplied by number of pleats per width*	×
Number of pleats per panel	=
Space Between Pleats	
Finished panel width (figured above)	
Overlap and return (figured left)	-
Width to be pleated	=
Divided by number of spaces per panel (one less than number of pleats per panel)	÷
Space between pleats	=
Pleat Size	
Flat width of hemmed panel (from step 3)	
Finished panel width (figured above)	-
Total amount allowed for pleats	=
Divided by number of pleats per panel (figured above)	÷
Pleat size	=

Figure 5 pleats per width of 48" (122 cm) fabric, 6 pleats per width of 54" (137 cm) fabric. For example, for 54" (137 cm) fabric, 3 widths per panel = 18 pleats. If you have a half width of fabric, figure 2 or 3 pleats in that half width.

LIST *of* MATERIALS

- ▶ Decorator fabric.
- ▶ Lining fabric, if desired.
- ▶ Buckram, 4" (10 cm) wide.
- ▶ Conventional or decorative traverse rod.
- ▶ Drapery weights; drapery hooks.

CUTTING DIRECTIONS

Use the Fabric Worksheet opposite to determine and record the necessary measurements. Several widths of fabric are often required. Cut the number of fabric widths you need to the calculated cut length of the draperies. If the number of widths is an odd number, divide one of the widths in half, and add one half to each of the two drapery panels.

1 ...... Seam widths together as necessary, removing selvages to prevent puckering; finish seam allowances by serging or zigzagging. Press seams open or to outer edge of drapery. At lower edge, press under 4" (10 cm) twice to wrong side; stitch to make double-fold hem, using blindstitch or straight stitch.

2 ...... Cut buckram the width of each drapery panel. Place buckram even with upper edge of drapery panel, on wrong side. Fold heading and buckram to wrong side; press. Fold again, encasing buckram in fabric; press. Pin or hand-baste in place.

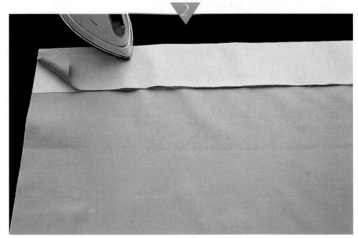

3 ...... Press under 1½" (3.8 cm) twice on sides. Tack drapery weights inside the side hems, about 3" (7.5 cm) from lower edge. Stitch double-fold side hems, using blindstitch or straight stitch; hand-stitch hem in place at heading. Determine the number and size of pleats and spaces between them as in Pleats Worksheet, opposite.

continued

4   Cut buckram templates in sizes to match determined pleats and spaces; cut five of each for 48" (122 cm) fabric or six of each for 54" (137 cm) fabric. Mark the overlap (o) and return (r), shown in step 5, on right side of one panel, using chalk. Arrange templates on first fabric width, with first pleat starting at overlap line and last pleat ending at seamline. There will be one less space. Adjust pleat sizes to arrange spaces evenly; spaces must remain uniform. Mark heading even with outer edges of space templates.

5   Arrange templates on second fabric width from overlap, with first space starting at first seamline from overlap and last pleat ending at next seamline; use same number of pleats as spaces. (Last pleat ends at return mark in last fabric width.) Adjust pleats as necessary; mark spaces. If return end of panel has a half width of fabric, plan for two pleats if the fabric is 48" (122 cm) wide or for three pleats if the fabric is 54" (137 cm) wide. Transfer markings to opposite panel in mirror-image placement.

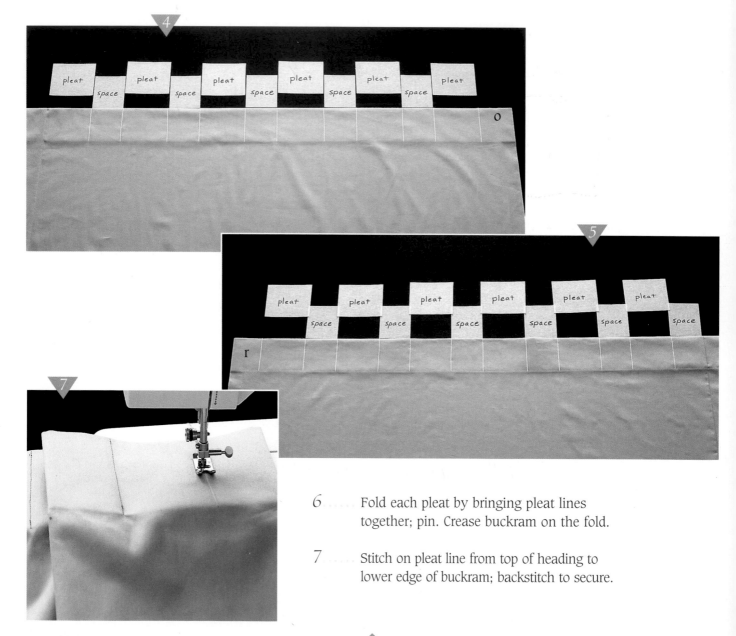

6   Fold each pleat by bringing pleat lines together; pin. Crease buckram on the fold.

7   Stitch on pleat line from top of heading to lower edge of buckram; backstitch to secure.

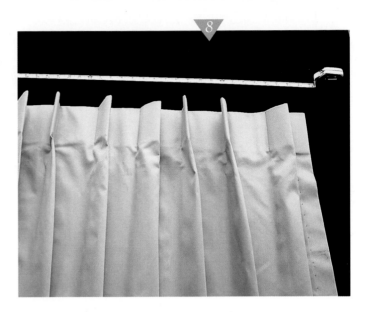

8 ..... Check finished width of panel along heading. Adjust size of a few pleats if necessary to adjust width of panel.

9 ..... Divide each stitched pleat into three even pleats. Open the pleat at the top of the heading. Pinch the folds of the pleats.

10 ..... Press center fold straight down to meet the pleat stitching line. Crease pleats that form at the sides.

11 ..... Pinch outer folds up to meet center fold. Finger-press three pleats together, making sure they are all even.

12 ..... Bar tack pleats by machine just above lower edge of buckram; or tack pleats by hand, using stabstitch and heavy-duty thimble.

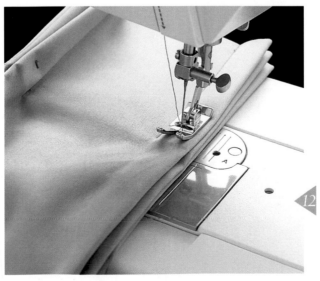

continued

13 .... Insert drapery hooks, with one hook at each pleat and one hook near each end of the panel. On a conventional traverse rod (a), top of hook is 1¾" (4.5 cm) from upper edge of overdrapery or 1¼" (3.2 cm) from upper edge of underdrapery. On a decorator traverse rod (b), top of hook is ¾" to 1" (2 to 2.5 cm) from upper edge. On a pole set with rings (c), top of hook is ¼" (6 mm) from upper edge. (Shown on traverse rods for clarity.)

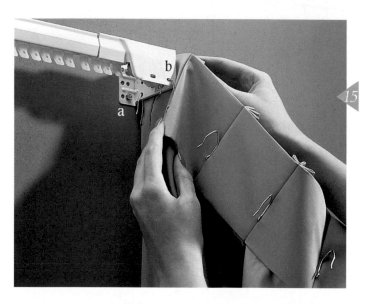

14 .... Crease the buckram midway between each pleat; fold it forward if a conventional traverse rod is being used, or fold it to the back if a decorative traverse rod is being used. This is often referred to as "cracking" the buckram. After cracking the buckram, press draperies, using warm, dry iron.

15 .... Hang the end hook at return in hole on the side of the bracket (a). Hang the hook of first pleat in hole at front corner of the bracket (b).

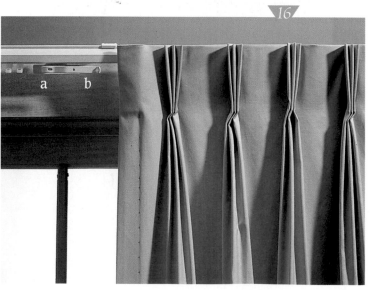

16 .... Hang the hooks for middle pleats on slides; remove any slides that are not used. Hang the hook for last pleat in first hole of master slide (a). Hang the end hook on overlap of drapery in end hole of master slide (b). Pinch the hooks on the master slides to keep them from catching when the draperies are drawn; also, pull the front master slide forward, if necessary.

17. . . . Open draperies completely into stacked position; check heading to be sure buckram is folded as it was cracked in step 14. Starting at heading, guide pleats into evenly spaced soft folds of equal depth; follow grainline of fabric to keep pleats perpendicular to floor.

18. . . . Staple narrow strip of matching fabric or muslin around drapery panel, midway between heading and hem, to hold pleats in place. Do not secure fabric too tightly, to prevent creasing the folds.

19. . . . Staple second strip of fabric at hemline. Check to see that draperies hang straight down from rod. Leave draperies in this position for two weeks to set the pleats. In humid conditions, one week may be sufficient.

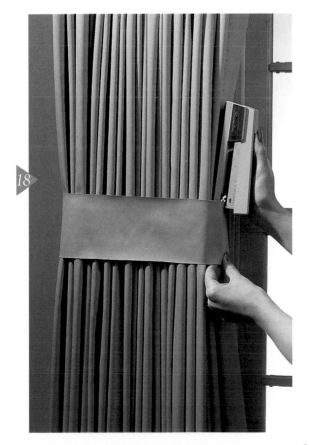

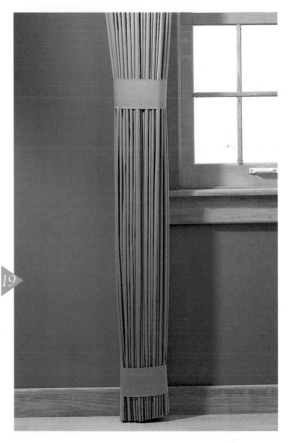

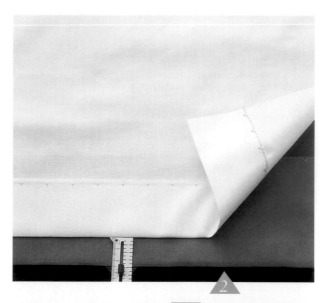

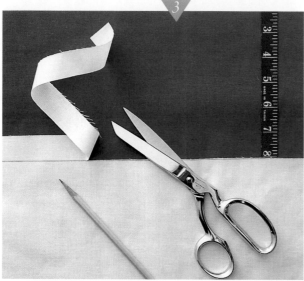

1..... Stitch drapery fabric as on page 33, step 1. Seam lining widths together as necessary, removing selvages to prevent puckering; finish seam allowances by serging or zigzagging, if desired. At lower edge, press under 2" (5 cm) twice to wrong side; stitch to make double-fold hem, using blindstitch or straight stitch.

2..... Place drapery panel on large flat surface. Lay lining panel on top of drapery panel, wrong sides together, with lower edge of lining 1" (2.5 cm) above lower edge of drapery panel; raw edges will be even at sides.

3..... Mark lining panel 8" (20.5 cm) from upper edge of drapery panel. Trim on marked line.

4..... Cut buckram the width of each drapery panel. Place buckram even with upper edge of drapery panel, on wrong side. Fold heading and buckram to wrong side; press.

5   Fold again, encasing the buckram in fabric; press. Lining edge will be even with the top of the heading. Pin or hand-baste in place.

6   Press under 1½" (3.8 cm) twice on sides, folding lining and drapery panels as one fabric. Tack the drapery weights inside the side hems, about 3" (7.5 cm) from lower edge.

7   Stitch double-fold side hems, using blind-stitch or straight stitch; hand-stitch side hem in place at heading.

8   Finish draperies as on pages 34 to 37, steps 4 to 19.

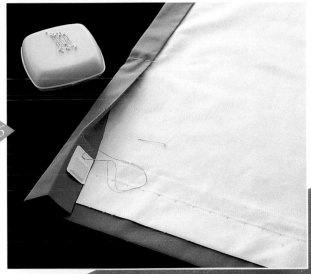

heading

Pleat VARIATIONS

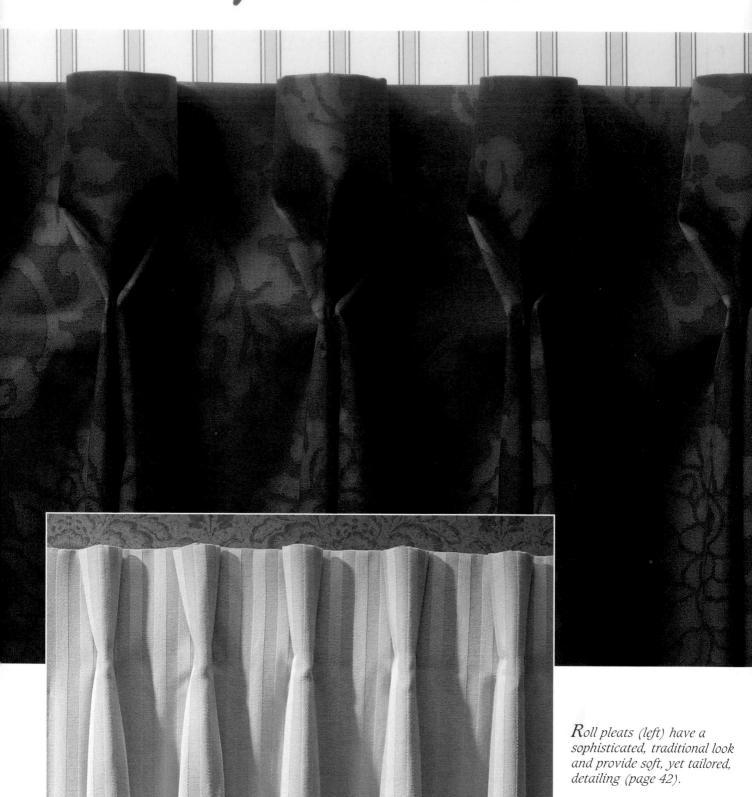

Roll pleats (left) have a sophisticated, traditional look and provide soft, yet tailored, detailing (page 42).

Double pinch pleats (above) have two pleats, instead of three, for a casual look (page 42).

Goblet pleats (left) give a soft look to the draperies (page 43). Because goblet pleats do not stack as tightly as pinch pleats, you may want to allow extra stackback (page 25) so the draperies will clear the window when open.

Grouped pleats (right) add interest to drapery headings. Achieve this look by sewing pleated draperies (page 31), varying the spacing between the pleats as on page 34, steps 4 and 5.

DRAPERIES WITH ROLL PLEATS

1...... Follow steps 1 to 8 on pages 33 to 35 for unlined draperies. Or for lined draperies, follow steps 1 to 7 on pages 38 and 39 and steps 4 to 8 on pages 34 and 35. Open the pleat at top of heading; holding two fingers under pleat, flatten pleat so it is centered over seamline.

2...... Roll sides of pleat so folded edges are even with stitching.

3...... Tack pleats as on page 35, step 12; position stitches near folded edge. Insert hooks and install draperies as on pages 36 and 37, steps 13 to 19.

HOW TO SEW DRAPERIES WITH DOUBLE PINCH PLEATS

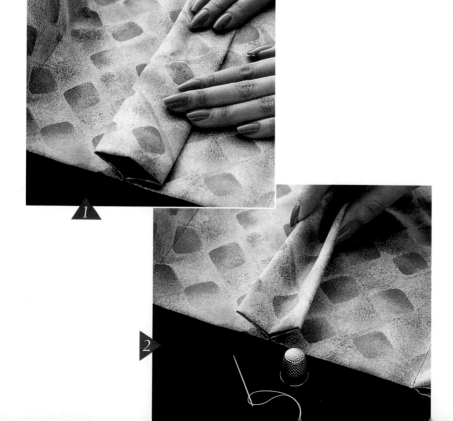

1...... Follow steps 1 to 8 on pages 33 to 35 for unlined draperies. Or for lined draperies, follow steps 1 to 7 on pages 38 and 39 and steps 4 to 8 on pages 34 and 35. Open the pleat at top of heading. Flatten pleat so it is centered over seamline.

2...... Bring folded edges up. Finger-press the two pleats together, making sure they are even. Tack pleats as on page 35, step 12. Insert hooks and install draperies as on pages 36 and 37, steps 13 to 19.

HOW TO SEW DRAPERIES WITH GOBLET PLEATS

1...... Follow steps 1 to 8 on pages 33
to 35 for unlined draperies. Or for
lined draperies, follow steps 1 to 7
on pages 38 and 39 and steps 4
to 8 on pages 34 and 35. Open
the pleat at top of heading. Pinch
fabric at bottom of buckram into
three or four small pleats.

2...... Tack pleats by hand, using stabstitch and heavy-duty thimble; or
bar tack pleats by machine just
above lower edge of buckram.

3...... Form pleat into rounded, goblet
shape. Hand-stitch pleat along
upper edge of drapery, as shown,
up to ½" (1.3 cm) on each side
of stitching line. Press draperies,
using warm, dry iron.

4...... Insert tissue paper into pleats, to
ensure that they retain goblet
shape. Insert hooks and install
draperies as on pages 36 and 37,
steps 13 to 19. Remove tissue
paper when draperies are cleaned.

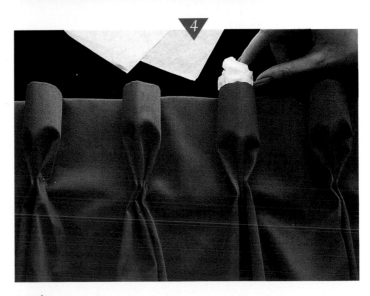

Self-styling CURTAINS

Curtains can be sewn quickly and easily, using self-styling tapes. The tape is applied flat to the top of the curtain panels, and the woven-in cords are pulled to create the heading of the curtain. For best results, use self-styling tapes on mediumweight to lightweight fabrics.

Self-styling tapes are available in various widths and styles. You may choose either sew-in or fusible tapes. Sew-in tapes are the most versatile, because they can be used for either lined or unlined curtains. Fusible tapes, however, work well for extra-quick, unlined curtains. On some fabrics, the fusible adhesive may affect the appearance of the curtain on the right side; test a piece of the fusible tape on the fabric you have selected before sewing the curtains.

Because most self-styling tapes form rather stiff headings, they are usually used for stationary window treatments. The curtains may be installed on standard or decorative curtain rods or on pole sets with rings. To hang panels from flat curtain rods, use drapery pins. Some tapes have loops woven into them for securing the drapery pins, and some manufacturers provide special pins for installation.

The amount of fullness needed in the curtain depends on the style of tape you select. Most tapes require two to three times fullness.

LIST *of* MATERIALS

▶ Decorator fabric.
▶ Lining fabric, if desired.
▶ Curtain rod or pole set with rings.
▶ Self-styling tape; use sew-in tape for unlined or lined curtains, or use fusible tape for unlined curtains.
▶ Drapery weights.

Smocking tape makes neatly smocked folds at the heading. For this bay window, two panels are held neatly in place with tiebacks.

Shirring tape creates a softly gathered heading that is consistent with the flowing fabric draped softly over a decorator pole.

Self-styling curtains are gathered by pulling the woven-in cords on the tape (right). Three styles are shown.

UNLINED CURTAINS USING SELF-STYLING TAPE

CUTTING DIRECTIONS

Allow for two to three times fullness, depending on the desired look and the type of self-styling tape. If a hand-draw pole set is used, determine the cut width of the decorator fabric by multiplying the length of the pole between brackets times the desired fullness and add 6" (15 cm) for each panel to allow for 1½" (3.8 cm) double-fold side hems. If it is necessary to piece fabric widths together to make each panel, also add 1" (2.5 cm) for each seam. If a standard or decorative curtain rod is used, also add twice the projection of the rod to this measurement to allow for returns.

If using a standard curtain rod, determine the finished length of the curtain by measuring from the top of the rod to where you want the lower edge of the drapery; then add ½" (1.3 cm) so the drapery will extend above the rod. Or if using a decorative curtain rod or a pole set with rings, measure from the pin holes in the slides or rings to the desired length. The cut length of the decorator fabric is equal to the desired finished length of the curtain plus ¾" (2 cm) for turn-under at the upper edge and 8" (20.5 cm) for a 4" (10 cm) double-fold hem at the lower edge.

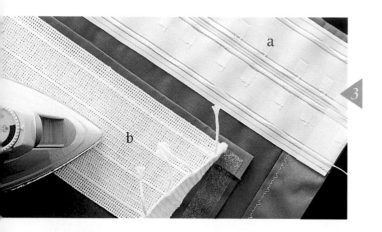

1 ...... Follow steps 1 and 3 on page 33; in step 3, omit reference to pleat spacing. Stitch side hems. Press under ¾" (2 cm) on upper edge of curtain panel.

2 ...... Cut shirring tape to width of hemmed panel plus 2" (5 cm). Turn under 1" (2.5 cm) on each end of tape, and use pin to pick out cords. Position tape right side up on wrong side of panel, with upper edge of tape ¼" (6 mm) from folded edge of panel.

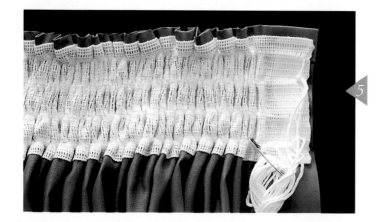

3 ...... Stitch sew-in tape (a) in place next to cords. Or fuse fusible tape (b) in place; then insert a strip of fusible web at ends along edges, and fuse.

4 ...... Knot all cords together, or knot them in pairs, at each end of shirring tape. At one end, pull evenly on cords to shirr fabric, adjusting width of heading to desired finished width.

5 ...... Knot cords in pairs at side of curtain. Cut off excess cord length, or conceal cords behind panel. If cords are not cut, panel can be smoothed for laundering.

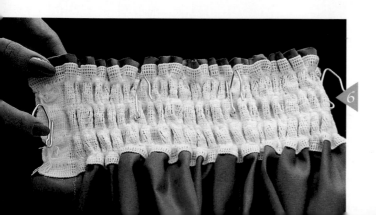

6 ...... Insert drapery pins at ends of panels and at 3" (7.5 cm) intervals. Or if self-styling tape has loops, insert drapery pins into them.

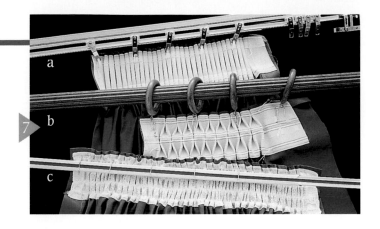

7...... Insert drapery pins into eyes of the slides on a decorative curtain rod (**a**) or eyes of rings for a pole set (**b**). Or hook pins over a standard curtain rod (**c**).

HOW TO SEW *L*INED CURTAINS USING SELF-STYLING TAPE

CUTTING DIRECTIONS

Determine the width and length of the decorator fabric as for unlined curtains, opposite. The cut width of the lining is equal to the cut width of the decorator fabric. The cut length of the lining is 5¾" (14.5 cm) shorter than the cut length of the decorator fabric; this allows for a 2" (5 cm) double-fold hem and for the lining to be 1" (2.5 cm) shorter than the finished curtain.

1...... Seam decorator fabric widths, if necessary, for each curtain panel; repeat for lining panel. At lower edge of curtain panel, press under 4" (10 cm) twice to wrong side; stitch to make double-fold hem. Repeat for lining panel, pressing under 2" (5 cm) twice.

2...... Press under ¾" (2 cm) on upper edge of curtain panel only. Place curtain panel and lining panel wrong sides together, matching raw edges at sides and with raw edge of lining at pressed foldline; fold edge of curtain panel over lining, and pin in place. At the bottom, the lining panel will be 1" (2.5 cm) shorter than the curtain panel.

3...... Press under 1½" (3.8 cm) twice on sides; tack drapery weights inside the side hems, about 3" (7.5 cm) from lower edge. Stitch to make double-fold hems. Finish the curtains as in steps 2 to 7, opposite.

Rod-pocket
BASICS

Rod-pocket curtains are often the choice when selecting a stationary window treatment that is stylish and easy to sew. Many different looks can be achieved with rod-pocket curtains, including interesting variations for headings (pages 54 and 55).

Several types of rods may be used for rod-pocket curtains, including flat rods in widths of 1", 2½", and 4½" (2.5, 6.5, and 11.5 cm). Wood and metal pole sets, used with elbows or finials, may also be used and are available in several diameters. Poles can also be created, using PVC pipe and fittings as on page 20.

When a pole set with elbows is used, the outer edges of the curtain panels wrap around the elbows to the wall. For curtains mounted on poles with finials, returns can be created by making an opening in the front of the rod pocket for inserting the pole.

Unlined rod-pocket curtains can be made from sheers or laces, creating a lightweight treatment that allows filtered light to enter the room. For curtains made from mediumweight to heavy-weight decorator fabrics, lining is used to make the curtains more durable, add extra body, and support the side hems and headings.

Before cutting the fabric, decide where the window treatment should be positioned and install the curtain rod or pole. Measure from the lower edge of the rod to where you want the lower edge of the curtain. To determine the finished length of the curtain, add the desired depth of the heading and rod pocket to this measurement. This is the finished length of the curtain panel from the top of the heading to the hemmed lower edge.

LIST *of* MATERIALS

▸ Decorator fabric.
▸ Lining fabric, optional.
▸ Drapery weights.
▸ Curtain rod or pole set with finials or elbows.
▸ Wooden brackets, keyhole brackets, or elbow brackets, for mounting pole.

Heading (**a**) is the portion at the top of a rod-pocket curtain that forms a ruffle when the curtain is on the rod. The depth of the heading is the distance from the top of the finished curtain to the top stitching line of the rod pocket.

Rod pocket (**b**) is the portion of the curtain where the curtain rod or pole is inserted; stitching lines at the top and bottom of the rod pocket keep the rod in place. To determine the depth of the rod pocket, measure around the widest part of the rod or pole; add ½" (1.3 cm) ease to this measurement, and divide by two.

Returns can be created for rod-pocket curtains that are mounted on poles with finials. The pole is inserted through an opening in the front of the rod pocket, allowing the side of the curtain to return to the wall.

CUTTING DIRECTIONS

Determine the depth of the rod pocket and heading (page 49) and the depth of the hem at the lower edge. A 4" (10 cm) double-fold hem is often used for the decorator fabric; if the curtain is lined, a 2" (5 cm) double-fold hem is used for the lining.

The cut length of the decorator fabric is equal to the desired finished length of the curtain plus the depth of the heading and the rod pocket plus ½" (1.3 cm) for turn-under at the upper edge plus twice the depth of the hem.

The cut width of the decorator fabric is determined by the length of the curtain rod, including the returns, multiplied by the amount of fullness desired in the curtain.

For sheer fabrics, allow two-and-one-half to three times the length of the rod for fullness; for heavier fabrics, allow two to two-and-one-half times. After multiplying the length of the rod times the desired fullness, divide this number by the number of panels being used for the treatment; add 6" (15 cm) for each panel to allow for 1½" (3.8 cm) double-fold side hems. If it is necessary to piece fabric widths together to make each panel, also add 1" (2.5 cm) for each seam.

Cut the lining fabric 5" (12.5 cm) shorter than the decorator fabric; the cut width of the lining is the same as the decorator fabric.

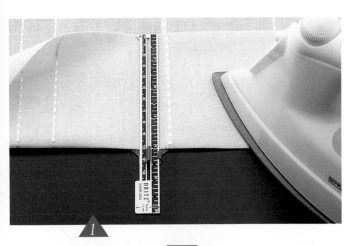

1 ...... Seam fabric widths, if necessary, for each curtain panel. At lower edge, press under an amount equal to the hem depth; repeat to press under a double-fold hem. Stitch, using straight stitch or blindstitch.

2 ...... Follow page 33, step 3, for side hems; omit reference to pleat spacing.

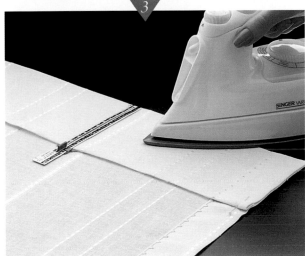

3 ...... Press under ½" (1.3 cm) on upper edge. Then press under an amount equal to rod-pocket depth plus heading depth. If curtains will be mounted on pole with elbow returns, omit steps 4 to 6.

4 ...... Mount rod on wooden, keyhole, or elbow bracket. Measure distance from the wall to center of the pole, as indicated by arrow.

5 ...... Unfold upper edge of curtain on return side of panel. On right side of fabric, measure from the hemmed edge of curtain a distance equal to the measurement in step 4; mark at center of rod pocket. If curtains will be mounted on rod with keyhole brackets, omit step 6.

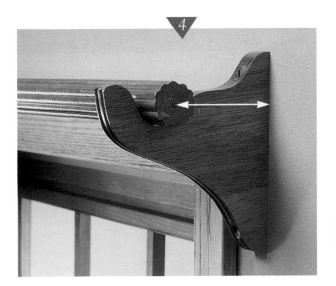

continued

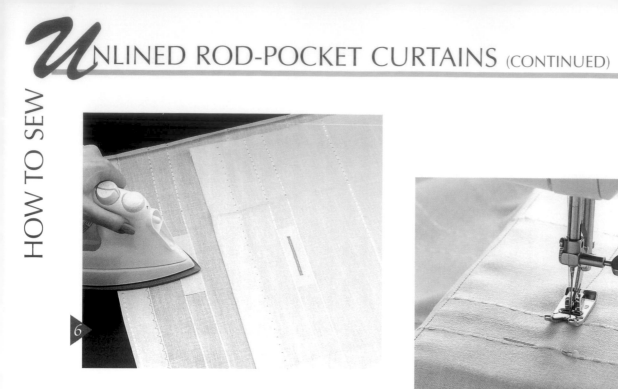

6...... Cut 1" (2.5 cm) strip of fusible interfacing, 1" (2.5 cm) longer than depth of the rod pocket, if the curtains will be mounted on a pole with wooden brackets. Fuse strip to wrong side of curtain panel, centering it directly under mark in step 5. On right side of panel, stitch a buttonhole at the mark, from top to bottom of rod pocket. Refold upper edge of panel along pressed lines; pin.

7...... Stitch close to first fold; stitch again at depth of heading, using tape on bed of sewing machine as stitching guide.

HOW TO SEW *L*INED
ROD-POCKET CURTAINS

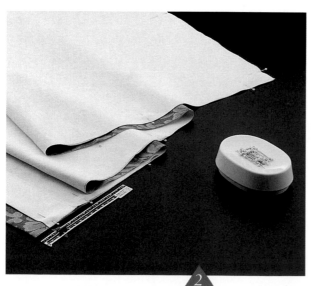

1...... Follow step 1 on page 51. Repeat for the lining, pressing under and stitching a 2" (5 cm) double-fold hem in the lining.

2...... Place curtain panel and lining panel wrong sides together, matching the raw edges at the sides and upper edge; pin. At the bottom, the lining panel will be 1" (2.5 cm) shorter than curtain panel. Complete the curtain as on page 51, steps 2 through 7, handling decorator fabric and lining as one fabric.

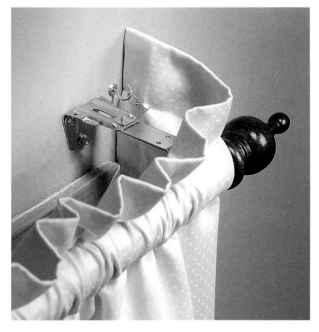

Pole with wooden brackets and finials. Remove the finials; insert pole into rod pocket with ends of the pole extending through the buttonholes. Reattach finials; mount pole. Secure return to the wooden bracket, using self-adhesive hook and loop tape.

Pole with keyhole bracket and finials. Slit center of the rod pocket at point marked in step 5 on page 51. Insert pole into rod pocket. Pull return over end of pole, aligning slit to finial screw hole; attach finials through slits, and mount pole. Attach a pin-on ring to inner edge of return, and secure to a cup hook or tenter hook in wall.

Pole with elbows. Insert the pole through the rod pocket; pull the curtain back to expose small screws. Mount the pole on brackets. Slide the curtain over brackets.

Decorative HEADINGS

Some simple variations in the headings of rod-pocket curtains can dramatically change their look. For some styles, such as the flounce heading or the popped heading, the variation is achieved by simply increasing the depth of the heading and arranging it after it has been installed. For styles such as the contrasting flounce and the welted heading, a separate facing is seamed to the curtain at the top of the heading. Although the instructions that follow are for lined curtains, the lining may be omitted, if desired, depending on the style of the curtain and the fabric selected.

Flounce heading drapes down over the front of the rod pocket, creating a mock valance. Allow a heading depth of 12" to 16" (30.5 to 40.5 cm). This treatment is suitable only for rods or poles with elbow returns. Sheer fabric may be used for this style in unlined curtains.

Popped heading is created by pulling the layers of the heading apart after inserting the rod into the pocket. Allow a heading depth of 6" to 8" (15 to 20.5 cm); do not press the upper edge of the curtain when turning under the heading and rod-pocket depth. This style may be used for sheer to medium-weight fabrics and may be lined or unlined.

Contrasting flounce can repeat a fabric that is used in the tieback for a coordinated look. A separate facing of contrasting fabric is sewn to the curtain at the top of the heading. Lining adds body to the heading and prevents show-through when a light-colored fabric is used for the flounce.

Welted heading, measuring 4" to 6" (10 to 15 cm) deep, droops into dramatic curves above the rod pocket. Contrasting welting is sewn into the seam at the top of the heading between the curtain and the facing. This style heading is appropriate for medium-weight fabrics and should always be lined.

ROD-POCKET CURTAINS WITH A FLOUNCE OR POPPED HEADING

LIST of MATERIALS

► Decorator fabric; lining.
► Drapery weights.
► Curtain rod or pole with elbow returns.

CUTTING DIRECTIONS

Cut the decorator fabric and lining as on page 50; allow for a 12" to 16" (30.5 to 40.5 cm) flounce heading, or a 6" to 8" (15 to 20.5 cm) popped heading.

Flounce heading. Sew curtains as on pages 51 and 52. When installing the curtains, drape the heading toward the front, over the rod pocket, and arrange the gathers.

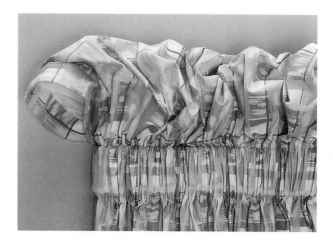

Popped heading. Sew curtains as on pages 50 to 52. Pull layers of heading apart, for a soft, rounded look.

HOW TO SEW ROD-POCKET CURTAINS WITH A CONTRASTING FLOUNCE

LIST of MATERIALS

► Decorator fabric.
► Contrasting decorator fabric, for facing.
► Lining.
► Drapery weights.
► Curtain rod or pole with elbow returns.

CUTTING DIRECTIONS

Cut the decorator fabric for the curtains with the length equal to the desired finished length of the curtains from the top of the curtain rod to the lower edge of the finished curtain plus twice the depth of the hem plus ½" (1.3 cm) for the seam allowance at the top plus the depth of the flounce heading; allow for a 12" to 16" (30.5 to 40.5 cm) flounce heading. Determine the cut width as on page 50.

Cut the fabric for the facing with the length equal to the depth of the heading plus the depth of the rod pocket plus 1" (2.5 cm) for turn-under and seam allowance. The cut width of the facing is the same as the cut width of the decorator fabric.

Cut the lining fabric 5" (12.5 cm) shorter than the decorator fabric. The cut width of the lining is the same as the cut width of the decorator fabric.

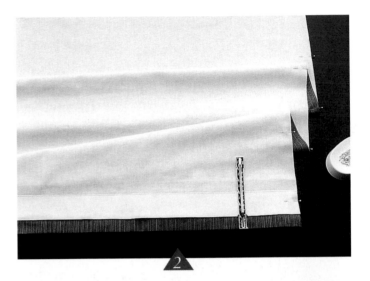

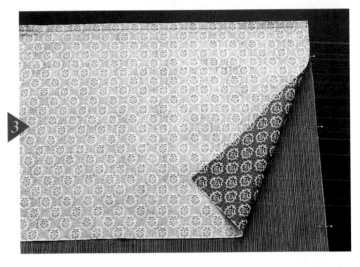

1...... Follow page 52, step 1.

2...... Place the curtain panel and the lining panel wrong sides together, matching the raw edges at sides and upper edge; pin. At the bottom, lining panel will be 1" (2.5 cm) shorter than the curtain panel.

3...... Pin facing to top of curtain panel, right sides together; if the facing fabric has one-way design, pin the flounce so design is upside down at the upper edge of the curtain panel. Stitch ½" (1.3 cm) seam; press the seam open.

4...... Press under 1½" (3.8 cm) twice on sides, folding lining and curtain fabric as one. Open out hem, and trim seam allowance in hem area. Tack drapery weights inside the side hems, about 3" (7.5 cm) from the lower edge. Stitch to make double-fold hems.

continued

ROD-POCKET CURTAINS WITH A CONTRASTING FLOUNCE (CONTINUED)

5...... Press under ½" (1.3 cm) on lower edge of flounce. Turn under facing along seamline; press. Pin flounce to the curtain panel along the lower pressed edge. Mark upper stitching line for rod pocket on facing. Pin along line to keep all layers together.

6...... Stitch close to lower pressed edge; stitch again along the marked line, creating rod pocket.

7...... Insert the rod or pole through rod pocket, gathering fabric evenly. Mount the rod or pole on brackets, draping heading toward the front, over the rod pocket, and arrange the gathers.

HOW TO SEW ROD-POCKET CURTAINS WITH A WELTED HEADING

LIST *of* MATERIALS

- ▶ Decorator fabric for curtain and facing.
- ▶ Contrasting fabric and ¼" (6 mm) cording, for covered welting.
- ▶ Lining fabric.
- ▶ Drapery weights.
- ▶ Curtain rod or pole set.

CUTTING DIRECTIONS

Cut the decorator fabric, facing, and lining as for rod-pocket curtains with a contrasting flounce (page 56); allow for a 4" to 6" (10 to 15 cm) heading. From contrasting fabric, cut bias fabric strips, 1⅝" (4 cm) wide, to cover the cording for the welting.

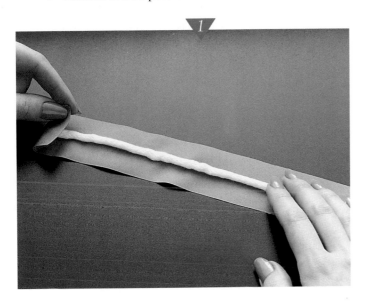

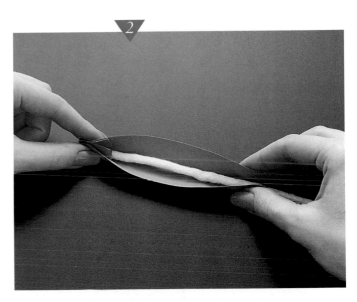

1 .... Seam the bias fabric strips together. Center the cording on the wrong side of the fabric strip, with the end of cording 1" (2.5 cm) from the end of strip; fold end of the strip back over the cording.

2 .... Fold the fabric strip around the cording, wrong sides together, matching the raw edges and encasing the end of the cording.

3 .... Machine-baste close to the cording, using a zipper foot, to create welting.

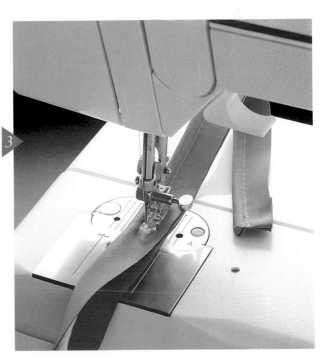

continued

4...... Follow steps 1 and 2 on page 57 for contrasting flounce. Stitch the welting to the right side of curtain panel at the upper edge, matching raw edges and stitching over the previous stitches; place encased end of welting 3" (7.5 cm) from side of panel. Stop stitching 5" (12.5 cm) from the opposite side of the panel.

5...... Mark the upper edge of the curtain 3" (7.5 cm) from the side; cut the welting 1" (2.5 cm) beyond the mark.

6...... Remove the stitching from end of welting, and cut the cording even with the mark on curtain panel.

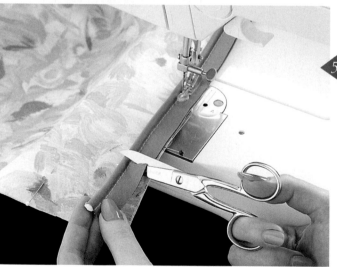

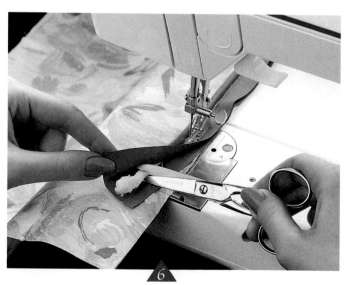

7...... Fold the end of fabric strip over the cording, encasing the end of the cording. Finish stitching welting to the curtain panel, ending 3" (7.5 cm) from the side.

8...... Follow steps 3 and 4 on page 57 for the contrasting flounce. When stitching side hems, stitch up to welting and secure threads; start stitching again on other side of the welting.

9...... Complete the curtains as on page 58, steps 5 and 6. Insert the rod or pole through the rod pocket, gathering the fabric evenly. Mount the rod or pole on brackets; arrange the heading in deep curves as desired.

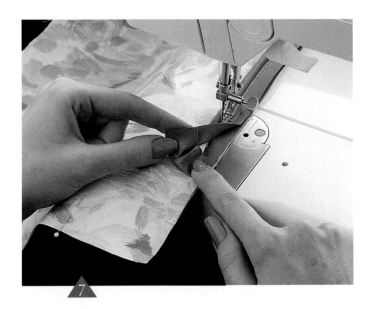

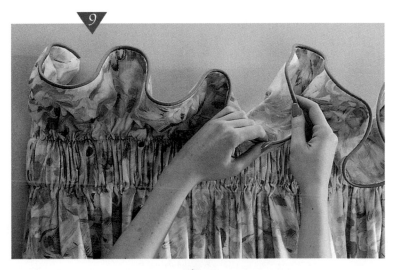

These unlined stationary rod-pocket curtains are made as two panels that meet in the center and share an attached valance. The panels can be held back at the sides with decorative hardware or fabric tiebacks. For best results,

Rod-pocket Curtains
WITH ATTACHED VALANCES

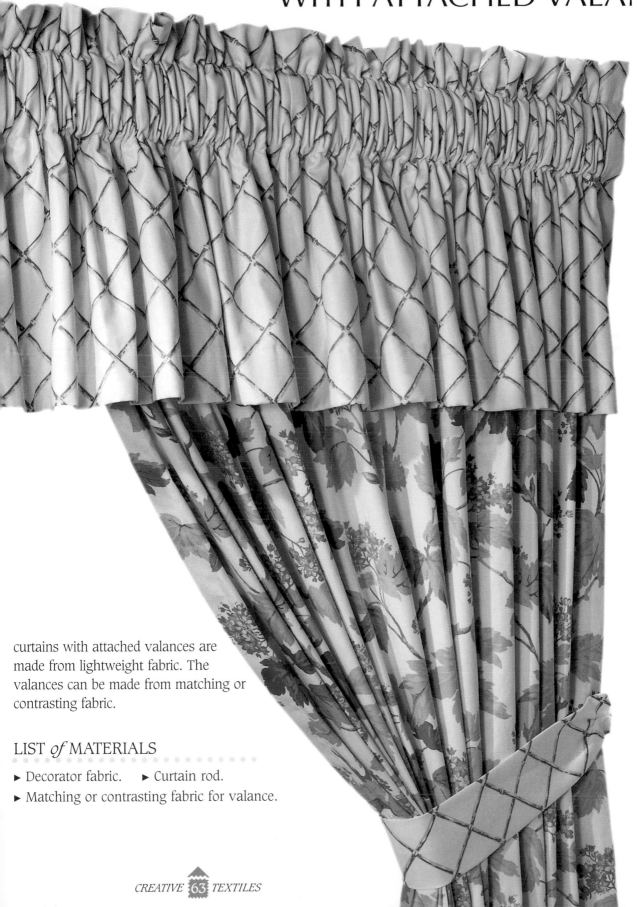

curtains with attached valances are made from lightweight fabric. The valances can be made from matching or contrasting fabric.

LIST of MATERIALS

- ▶ Decorator fabric.
- ▶ Curtain rod.
- ▶ Matching or contrasting fabric for valance.

CUTTING DIRECTIONS

Determine the desired finished length of the curtain from the top of the heading to the hemmed lower edge. Also decide on the depth of the rod pocket and the heading. The rod pocket is one-half the measurement around the rod plus 1/4" (6 mm); lower hems may be 3" (7.5 cm) for window curtains and 2" (5 cm) for a valance.

The cut length of the fabric for the curtain panels is equal to the desired finished length of the curtain plus twice the hem depth. Determine the cut width of the fabric for the curtain panels by multiplying the length of the rod by two and one-half; if you are sewing two curtain panels, divide this measurement by two to determine the cut width of each panel. For each panel, add 4" (10 cm) to allow for two 1" (2.5 cm) double-fold side hems; if it is necessary to piece fabric widths together, also add 1" (2.5 cm) for each seam.

Determine the desired finished length of the valance from the top of the heading to the hemmed lower edge. The cut length of the fabric for the valance is equal to the desired finished length of the valance plus the depth of the heading and rod pocket, 1/2" (1.3 cm) for turn-under at the upper edge, and twice the hem depth.

The cut width of the valance is equal to the finished width of the curtain plus 4" (10 cm) for the side hems; also add 1" (2.5 cm) for each seam. If two curtain panels are to be attached to the same valance, base the cut width of the valance on the combined finished width of the curtain panels.

1...... Seam fabric widths and stitch the lower hems of the curtain panels and valance as on page 33, step 1, using desired hem depth. Stitch 1" (2.5 cm) double-fold side hems.

2...... Press under 1/2" (1.3 cm) on upper edge of the valance. Then press under an amount equal to the rod-pocket depth plus heading depth.

3...... Place the valance right side down on a flat surface; open out upper fold. Place the curtain panels over valance, right side down, aligning upper edge of curtain with foldline on valance. Refold the upper edge of the valance, encasing upper edge of curtain; pin in place.

4 ...... Stitch close to the first fold. Stitch again at depth of heading, using tape on bed of machine as stitching guide. Insert curtain rod through rod pocket, gathering fabric evenly. Hang curtain.

Rounded-rod CURTAINS

Wide, rounded curtain rods, such as Continental® Plus and Pinnacle®, add dimension and depth to a rod-pocket curtain. To make a rod-pocket curtain for a rounded rod, make the front of the rod pocket deeper than the back, to allow for the "D" shape of the rod.

LIST *of* MATERIALS

▸ Decorator fabric.

▸ Rounded curtain rod.

CUTTING DIRECTIONS

To determine the finished length of the curtain, measure from the bottom of the rod to where you want the lower edge of the curtain; then add the desired heading depth and the depth of the *back* rod pocket.

The cut length of each curtain panel is equal to the finished length plus the depth of the heading, the depth of the *front* rod pocket, twice the width of the hem, and 1/2" (1.3 cm) for turn-under. Determine the cut width of the curtain as on page 50, except add 4" (10 cm) for 1" (2.5 cm) double-fold side hems instead of 6" (15 cm).

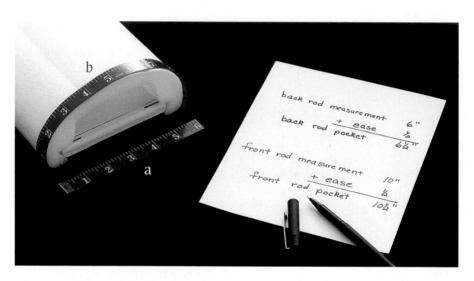

Determine the depth of the back rod pocket (a) by measuring the back, flat portion of the rod; add 1/2" (1.3 cm) ease to this measurement. Determine the depth of the front rod pocket (b) by measuring around the front, rounded portion of the rod; add 1/2" (1.3 cm) ease to this measurement.

1 ...... Follow step 1 on page 51 for rod-pocket curtains. Press under 1/2" (1.3 cm) at upper edge of curtain panel. From foldline, measure a distance equal to the back rod pocket plus the heading depth; press.

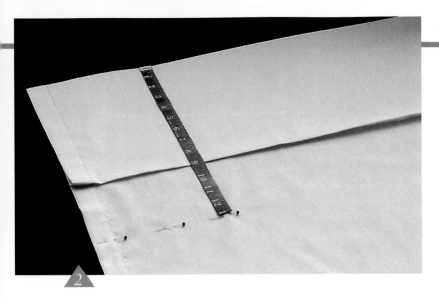

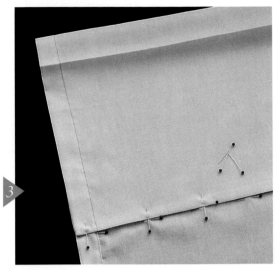

2...... Measure a distance equal to heading depth plus front rod pocket from second foldline; pin-mark on wrong side of fabric.

3...... Align first foldline to pin marks; pin fabric layers together. Stitch close to foldline.

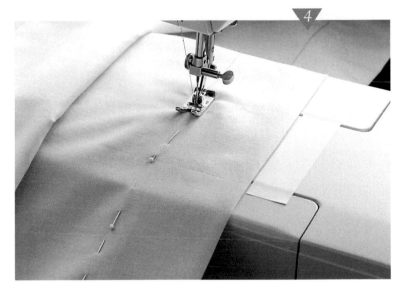

4...... Refold panel at second foldline. Mark heading depth from foldline; stitch rod pocket. As a guide for stitching, apply masking tape to sewing machine bed.

5...... Insert curtain rod into rod pocket. Install rod on brackets.

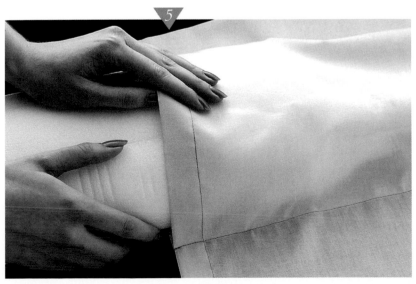

MORE IDEAS FOR
Rod-pocket
CURTAINS

*V*alances are shorter versions of rod-pocket curtains (page 49) with 1¹/₂" (3.8 cm) double-fold hems at the lower edges. When using a valance over curtains, install it on a separate curtain rod. When using a valance between two side panels of curtains, install it on the same curtain rod.

*T*ieback curtains are rod-pocket panels (page 49), pulled back and held in place with tiebacks. For a new look, use craft ornaments, costume jewelry, silk flowers, or tassels as the tiebacks.

*B*ishop sleeve curtains (opposite) are rod-pocket curtains that are elegantly pouffed. The fabric at the bottom of these extra-long curtain panels puddles lavishly onto the floor.

Curtains with trimmed rod pockets have decorative cording or gimp along the rod pockets. Apply the trim to the installed curtain, using pressure-sensitive adhesive or double-stick carpet tape, trimmed to size.

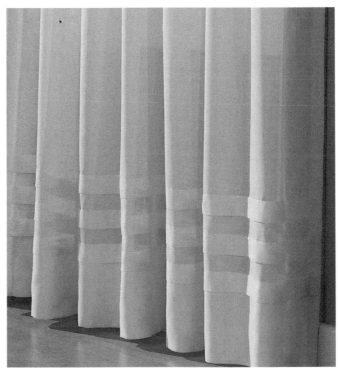

Tucked curtains (page 71) feature tucks near the lower edge.

BISHOP SLEEVE CURTAINS

LIST *of* MATERIALS

▸ Decorator fabric.
▸ Curtain rod; tenter hooks or cup hooks.
▸ Cording; bodkin or safety pin.
▸ Tissue paper, optional.

CUTTING DIRECTIONS

Cut two curtain panels, using one fabric width for each panel. Calculate the cut length of each panel as for rod-pocket curtains on page 50, allowing 2" (5 cm) for a 1" (2.5 cm) double-fold hem at the lower edge; add an extra 12" (30.5 cm) of length for each pouf and 12" (30.5 cm) to puddle on the floor.

1 ...... Press under 1" (2.5 cm) twice on sides of panel; stitch. Repeat for hem at lower edge. Stitch rod pocket and heading as on pages 51 and 52, steps 3 to 7.

2 ...... Insert a cord into hem at lower edge, using bodkin or safety pin. Pull cord tightly to gather lower edge.

3 ...... Insert curtain rod through rod pockets, gathering fabric evenly. Install rod on brackets. Determine location of poufs by tightly bunching panel with hands and lifting it to desired position.

4 ...... Attach tenter hook or cup hook behind each pouf to hold tieback. Secure tieback tightly. Tuck tissue paper into pouf, if desired, to improve blousing.

5 ...... Arrange bottom of bishop sleeve curtain, puddling fabric onto floor.

LIST *of* MATERIALS

► Lightweight or sheer decorator fabric.
► Curtain rod.

CUTTING DIRECTIONS

Cut rod-pocket curtain panels as on page 50, allowing 16" (40.5 cm) for an 8" (20.5 cm) double-fold hem at the lower edge; add 9" (23 cm) of length for three tucks.

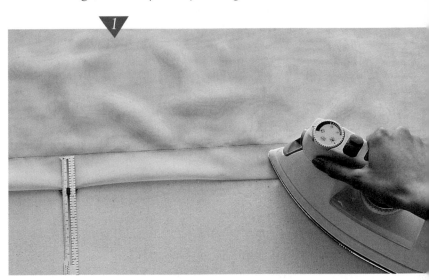

1...... Seam fabric widths, if necessary, for each curtain panel. At lower edge, press under 8" (20.5 cm) twice to wrong side; stitch to make double-fold hem. With wrong sides of fabric together, press foldline for tuck 1⅝" (4 cm) from upper edge of hem.

2...... Press second foldline 6" (15 cm) away from first foldline; press third foldline 6" (15 cm) away from second foldline.

3...... Stitch the tucks 1½" (3.8 cm) from foldlines. For easier stitching, place tape on bed of sewing machine to use as a guide. Press tucks toward lower edge. Press under 1" (2.5 cm) twice on sides. Stitch to make double-fold side hems. Complete curtain, following pages 51 and 52, steps 3 to 7.

Unlined
TAB CURTAINS

Versatile tab curtains offer a variety of looks with either long or short tabs. The unlined panels are constructed with a facing at the upper edge. If desired, the facing can be cut from contrasting fabric and folded to the front of the panel for a banded effect. The facing strip should have a finished width of 1" (2.5 cm) or wider if a contrasting band is desired.

Hang the curtains from a decorative pole set, or, for a unique look, hang them from decorative knobs inserted into the woodwork above the window. The pole set may be mounted on or above the window frame, depending on the desired look.

Decorative knobs are available in many styles and finishes. Some styles include screws suitable for inserting into the woodwork. Other knobs, intended for use with a bolt, can be secured to woodwork using hanger bolts (page 75). These bolts, available at specialty woodworking stores, have a metal thread at one end for inserting them into the knob, and a wood thread at the opposite end for inserting into the woodwork. Knobs are generally mounted 4" to 10" (10 to 25.5 cm) apart, depending on the size of the window and the amount of drape desired. To avoid splitting the woodwork, predrill holes before inserting the knobs.

Tab curtains can be designed for a variety of looks. The tab curtains at left have a coordinating band at the upper edge and are mounted on a pole. The tab curtain opposite hangs from decorative knobs and is pulled to the side with a length of cording.

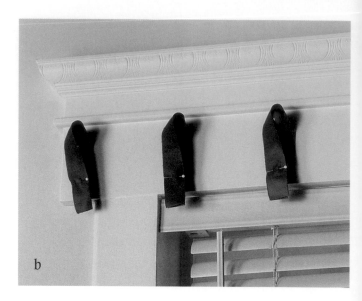

Determine the tab length by pinning fabric strips over pole or rod (**a**) or around knob (**b**); mark tab at the desired distance, using pins. The tabs may be 4" to 8" (10 to 20.5 cm) in length.

HOW TO SEW *U*NLINED TAB CURTAINS

LIST *of* MATERIALS

▶ Lightweight to mediumweight decorator fabric.

▶ Decorative pole set or knobs.

▶ Hanger bolts, if necessary, for securing knobs to woodwork.

CUTTING DIRECTIONS

Determine the desired finished length of the curtain by measuring from the bottom of the pole or knob to the desired finished hem; then subtract the amount of space, or distance, desired between the lower edge of the pole or knob and the upper edge of the curtain.

The cut length of the curtain is equal to the desired finished length of the curtain plus 2½" (6.5 cm) to allow for a 1" (2.5 cm) double-fold hem at the lower edge and a ½" (1.3 cm) seam allowance at the upper edge.

The cut width of the curtain is equal to one-and-one-half to two times the length of the pole or width of the window. If you are sewing two curtain panels, divide this measurement by two to determine the cut width of each panel. For each panel, add 4" (10 cm) to allow for 1"

(2.5 cm) double-fold side hems. If it is necessary to piece fabric widths together to make each panel, also add 1" (2.5 cm) for each seam.

Determine the spacing and the number of tabs for each curtain panel. The tabs are spaced from 6" to 12" (15 to 30.5 cm) apart, depending on the amount of fullness or drape desired between the tabs. Determine the tab length (above). Cut two 1¼" (3.2 cm) strips of fabric for each tab to the determined measurement, adding ½" (1.3 cm) at each end for seam allowances.

Cut the facing strip twice the desired width plus 1" (2.5 cm) for seam allowances. The cut length of the facing strip is equal to the cut width of the panel; piece strips together as necessary for the desired length.

Decorative knobs that have screws with a wood thread at one end are suitable for inserting into woodwork. Knobs that have screws without a wood thread (a) can be made suitable for inserting into woodwork by replacing the screw with a hanger bolt (b). Hanger bolts have a metal thread at one end for inserting into the knob and a wood thread at the opposite end for inserting into the woodwork.

1   Stitch fabric widths together for each panel, stitching ½" (1.3 cm) seams. Finish the seams. At lower edge of the panel, press under 1" (2.5 cm) twice to wrong side of panel; stitch, using straight stitch or blindstitch, to make double-fold hem.

2   Place two tab strips right sides together, matching raw edges. Stitch ¼" (6 mm) seam on long edges. Repeat for remaining tabs. Turn tabs right side out, and press.

3   Fold tabs in half as shown opposite for knob or pole mount. Pin to upper edge of curtain panel, matching raw edges. Pin tabs to right side of panel if facing will be folded to wrong side; pin tabs to wrong side of panel if facing will be folded to the right side for contrasting band. Place tabs at ends 2" (5 cm) from each side; space remaining tabs evenly between the end tabs. Machine-baste tabs in place.

4   Fold the facing strip in half lengthwise, wrong sides together; press. Pin the facing to right side of panel at upper edge, matching raw edges; or, for contrasting band, pin to wrong side of panel. Stitch ½" (1.3 cm) seam at upper edge; trim to ¼" (6 mm).

5   Press the facing to wrong side of panel; or, for contrasting band, press the band to right side. Topstitch close to upper edge and folded edge of facing or band.

6   Press under 1" (2.5 cm) twice at the sides. Stitch to make double-fold hems, using a straight stitch or blindstitch.

7   Hang the curtain panel from knobs or from a decorative pole set.

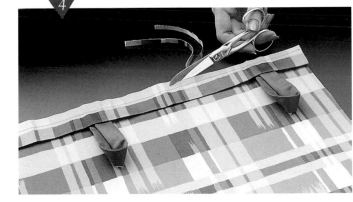

Lined Tie-tab CURTAINS

For an informal look, make tie-tab curtains. Used with a pole set or decorative curtain rod, this simple, no-fuss curtain has plenty of style. Lined tie-tab curtains drape well and are easy to sew. The size of the tabs and the spacing between them may vary, depending on the look you want.

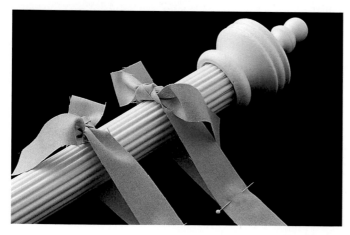

Determine tab length by pinning fabric strips over pole or rod, with tabs tied in knot or bow as desired; mark tab at desired distance from pole, using pins. Untie, and cut strips to marked length plus ¾" (2 cm) to allow for seam allowances.

LIST *of* MATERIALS

▸ Decorator fabric and lining fabric, for curtain panels.
▸ Matching or contrasting fabric, for tabs.
▸ Pole set or decorative curtain rod.
▸ Drapery weights.

CUTTING DIRECTIONS

Determine the finished length of the curtain by measuring from the bottom of the pole or rod to where you want the lower edge of the curtain; then subtract the distance or space you want between the bottom of the pole and the upper edge of the curtain. Determine the width of the hem at the lower edge. A 4" (10 cm) double-fold hem is often used for the decorator fabric and a 2" (5 cm) double-fold hem for the lining.

The cut length of the decorator fabric is equal to the desired finished length of the curtain plus twice the width of the hem plus ½" (1.3 cm) for the seam allowance at the upper edge.

The cut width of the decorator fabric is equal to two or two-and-one-half times the length of the pole or rod. After multiplying the length of the pole times the desired fullness, add 6" (15 cm) for each panel to allow for 1½" (3.8 cm) double-fold side hems. If it is necessary to piece fabric widths together to make each panel, also add 1" (2.5 cm) for each seam.

The cut length of the lining is 5" (12.5 cm) shorter than the cut length of the decorator fabric; this allows for a 2" (5 cm) double-fold hem at the lower edge and for the lining to be 1" (2.5 cm) shorter than the curtain when it is finished. The cut width of the lining is equal to the cut width of the decorator fabric.

Decide on the finished width you want the tabs to be. Then determine the spacing and number of tabs for each curtain panel; two tabs are placed at each location. Evenly space the tabs 3" to 8" (7.5 to 20.5 cm) apart, depending on the look you want.

Cut one strip of decorator fabric and one of matching or contrasting fabric for each tab, with each fabric strip ½" (1.3 cm) wider and ¾" (2 cm) longer than the desired finished size.

HOW TO SEW *L*INED TIE-TAB CURTAINS

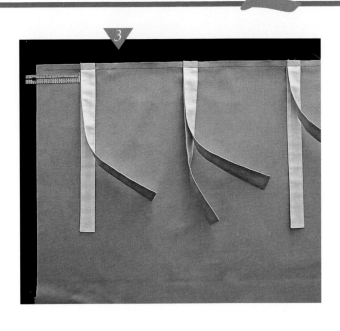

1...... Place two tab strips right sides together, matching raw edges. Stitch ¼" (6 mm) seam around long sides and one end of tab. Repeat for remaining tabs. Trim corners, turn tabs right side out, and press.

2...... Follow page 38, step 1.

3...... Pin tabs to right side of curtain panel at upper edge, with raw edges matching and right sides of tabs facing down; place two tabs at each placement. Tabs at ends must be placed 3" (7.5 cm) from each side; space remaining tabs evenly between the end tabs. Machine-baste the tabs in place.

4...... Place curtain panel and lining panel right sides together, matching raw edges at sides and upper edge; pin. At the bottom, the lining panel will be 1" (2.5 cm) shorter than the curtain panel.

5...... Stitch ½" (1.3 cm) seam at upper edge. Press seam allowances open; then fold lining to wrong side of curtain, and press.

6...... Follow page 39, steps 6 and 7.

7...... Tie knots or bows around pole or rod. Install pole on brackets.

MORE IDEAS FOR *Lined Tie-tab* CURTAINS

Tailored tabs give a look of simplicity to this curtain. Instead of tying the tabs, insert both ends into the seam at the upper edge of the curtain. One tab is inserted at each placement mark; the finished size of the tabs shown here is 2½" × 9" (6.5 × 23 cm). The space between the tabs is 4½" (11.5 cm).

Alternating tabs (left) are tied together to create the uniform, soft folds. The curtain has two-and-one-half times fullness. Only one tab is inserted at each placement mark on this curtain; the finished size of the tabs shown here is 1½" × 11" (3.8 × 28 cm). An even number of tabs is used for this curtain, and the space between the tabs is 3" (7.5 cm).

Knotted tabs (opposite) in two colors are tied close to the curtains for a new look. The finished size of the tabs that wrap around the pole is 1½" × 15" (3.8 × 38 cm); the front tabs are 3" (7.5 cm) shorter. The space between the tabs is 6" (15 cm).

Simple CURTAIN PANELS

Simple curtain panels hung from decorative rods can take on an elegant or casual look, depending on the choice of fabric and curtain hardware used. The curtains can be made with side returns, if desired, to block out the side light and view. Unlined panels can be trimmed with an optional edging on the inner edge of the panel or can be made with an attached flounce. Stitch fringe, grosgrain ribbon, or other trim to the lower edge of the flounce, if desired, for embellishment. These panels may be made to hang even across the top, or they may be made so the fabric swoops between the curtain rings with excess length puddling on the floor. For a tailored effect that produces a firm upper edge, buckram can be used to provide stiffening. For sheers or light-weight fabrics designed to swoop between the rings, the buckram is omitted.

Lined curtain panels can take on a formal or casual look. For a tailored appearance, make them with a decorative welting stitched between the layers along the inner edges of the curtain panels. Use a coordinating fabric for the lining, because a small amount of it will show when the curtain is tied back. The lined curtain panels can be made with a short flounce, if desired, and the flounce can be gathered up at each ring and stitched to create a scalloped effect, if desired.

For a sheer treatment, make a double-layer sheer that hangs from decorative rings or tabs. The sheer provides a soft, drapable look, and the double layer provides more privacy. For interest, layer two colored sheers or a white sheer over a colored sheer.

The amount of fullness can affect the look of the curtain panels. The amount of drape across the top of the panels can be varied by the number of rings used as well as by the spacing between them. Hem allowances are determined based on the length of the curtain and the weight and drapability of the fabric used. For firm fabrics, you may want to use a 4" (10 cm) double-fold hem at the lower edge and 1½" (3.8 cm) side hems. For sheer or lightweight draped fabrics, or for short curtains, you may want to use 1" (2.5 cm) double-fold hems for both the lower and side edges. Use a ⅜" (1 cm) double-fold hem on the inner edge of curtains and lower edges of flounces edged with braid trim or fringe.

UNLINED CURTAIN PANELS

LIST *of* MATERIALS

▶ Decorator fabric in weight suitable for desired style.

▶ Braid, ribbon, or fringe trim for inner edge of curtain or lower edge of flounce, optional.

▶ Decorator rod and sew-on rings.

▶ Buckram, optional.

▶ Pin-on rings and cup hooks or tenter hooks, for securing returns to wall, for curtains with returns.

CUTTING DIRECTIONS

For unlined curtain panels, determine the desired finished length of the panels. To determine the cut length, add 7" (18 cm) for 3½" (9 cm) double-fold hem at the upper edge and from 2" to 8" (5 to 20.5 cm) for double-fold hem at the lower edge, depending on the desired hem allowance, plus 12" to 20" (30.5 to 51 cm) for puddling on the floor, if desired.

Decide on the desired fullness of the panels. Multiply the length of the rod including side returns, if desired, times the desired fullness; divide this amount by the width of the fabric to determine the number of fabric widths required. Use full or half widths of fabric.

For unlined curtain panels with attached flounces, follow the instructions above for unlined curtain panels, adding 2" (5 cm) for a 1" (2.5 cm) double-fold hem at the upper edge instead of 7" (18 cm). For a plain attached flounce, cut a length of fabric 4" (10 cm) longer than the desired finished length of the flounce, or for an edged flounce, 2¾" (7 cm) longer than the desired finished length of the flounce. The finished length of the flounce is generally about 15" (38 cm), but can be shorter or longer, depending on the desired finished look. Seam flounce widths together as in step 1, opposite, for curtain widths. Trim the flounce to the same width as the curtain panels.

Formal floor-length curtain panels (right) are trimmed with soft fringe. The more casual curtain (below) has a flounce edged with eyelet and ribbon.

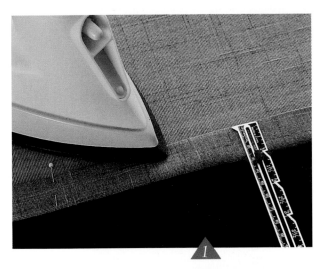

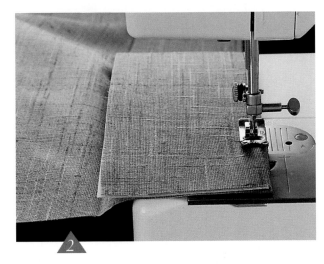

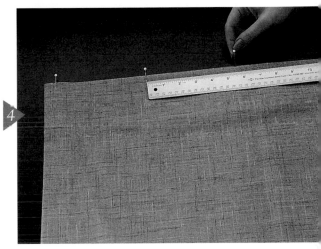

1 .... Seam the fabric widths as necessary, removing selvages to prevent puckering. Finish seam allowances by serging or zigzagging. At lower edge, press up desired hem allowance twice to wrong side; stitch to make double-fold hem, using blindstitch or straight stitch.

2 .... Stabilize upper edge, if desired, with a 3½" (9 cm) strip of buckram cut to the width of each curtain panel. Place buckram even with upper edge of curtain panel, on wrong side. Fold heading and buckram to wrong side; press. Fold again, encasing buckram in fabric; press. Pin along first foldline, and stitch ¼" (6 mm) from edge, as shown. Refold along second foldline.

3 .... Press under 1½" (3.8 cm) twice on outer edge of curtain panel. Stitch double-fold side hem, using blindstitch or straight stitch. For plain curtain panels, repeat on inner edge. For panels edged in trim, fold under ⅜" (1 cm) twice to wrong side and stitch close to folded edge. Pin or glue-baste decorative trim to inner edge of curtain panel, and stitch close to both edges of trim. Fold 1" (2.5 cm) to wrong side at upper and lower edges; hand-stitch in place.

4 .... Plan and pin-mark spacing for rings at top of curtain panel. If fewer rings are used, spaced farther apart, more fabric drapes between them. For a more controlled look, use more rings, spaced closer together.

continued

UNLINED CURTAIN PANEL (CONTINUED)

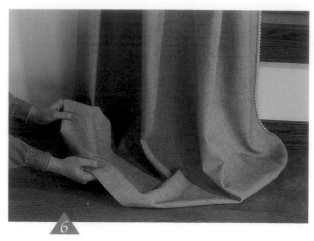

5...... Check the drape of the panel by securing it at pin marks to the side of an ironing board, with markings spaced the desired distance apart. Adjust number of rings and spacing between them, if necessary. Attach sew-on rings.

6...... Hang panels from decorative rod, using rings. For curtains with returns, attach pin-on ring to the inner edge of return and secure to a tenter hook or cup hook in wall. Arrange excess fabric to puddle on the floor, if curtain was designed to puddle.

HOW TO SEW AN UNLINED CURTAIN PANEL WITH AN ATTACHED FLOUNCE

1...... Follow page 83, step 1, for curtain panel and flounce; use a 1" (2.5 cm) double-fold hem at the lower edge of a plain flounce or a ³⁄₈" (1 cm) double-fold hem at the lower edge of a trimmed flounce. Stitch double-fold hems on sides of curtain and flounce panels. If using trim, pin or glue-baste trim to the lower edge of flounce. Stitch close to both edges of trim. Fold about 1" (2.5 cm) of trim to wrong side at ends; hand-stitch in place.

2...... Pin flounce to curtain panel, right sides up, at upper edges. Stitch 2" (5 cm) from raw edges; press seam allowance toward curtain panel. Trim facing hem allowance of curtain panel ¹⁄₄" (6 mm) from stitching. Fold 1" (2.5 cm) at upper edge of flounce to wrong side; pin. Stitch close to folded edge. Continue as on page 83, steps 4 to 6.

LINED CURTAIN PANELS

LIST of MATERIALS

- ► Decorator fabric for curtain and lining.
- ► Welting, optional (page 59).
- ► Decorative rod and rings.

CUTTING DIRECTIONS

For lined curtain panels, cut the curtain and lining following the instructions for unlined panels on page 82, adding ½" (1.3 cm) for the seam allowance at the upper edge, instead of 7" (18 cm) for the hem allowance.

For lined curtain panels with attached flounces, cut the curtain and lining following the instructions for unlined panels on page 82, except use ½" (1.3 cm) seam allowance on both sides of the curtain and add ½" (1.3 cm) for the seam allowance at the upper edge plus 2½" to 8" (6.5 to 20.5 cm) for an attached flounce.

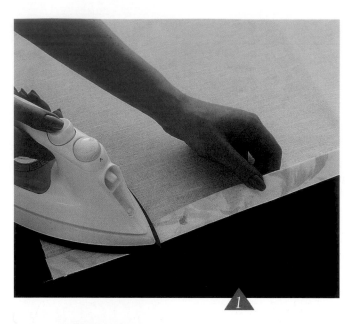

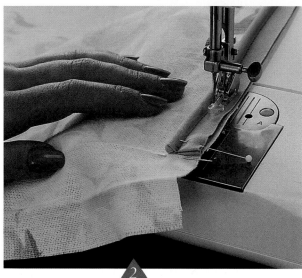

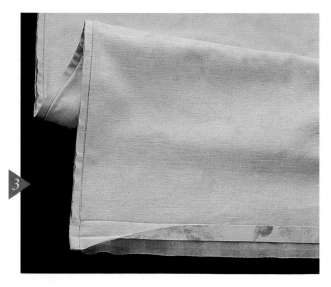

1 . . . . . . Seam the fabric widths as necessary, removing selvages to prevent puckering. At lower edge, press up desired hem allowance twice to wrong side and mark finished curtain length with pin.

2 . . . . . . Make welting as on page 59, steps 1 to 3, if desired, and stitch welting to right side of inner edge of curtain panel with raw edges aligned; place encased end of welting just beyond seam allowance at upper edge. At remaining end, cut the welting 1" (2.5 cm) beyond the finished length of the curtain. Continue as on pages 60 and 61, steps 6 and 7; in step 7, omit reference to ending 3" (7.5 cm) from side. If using decorative welting, turn welting into seam allowance ½" (1.3 cm) from upper edge and at marked finished length at lower edge.

3 . . . . . . Pin curtain and lining right sides together along inner edge. Stitch just inside previous stitching on a curtain edged with welting, extending stitching to upper and lower raw edges of panels. Or for a panel with no edging, stitch ½" (1.3 cm) from raw edges.

4...... Stabilize upper edge, if desired, with a 3½" (9 cm) strip of buckram cut to the width of each curtain panel. Place buckram even with upper edge of curtain panel, on wrong side, from seam allowance at inner edge to raw edge at outer edge; pin curtain panel, lining, and buckram together through all layers. Stitch ½" (1.3 cm) from upper raw edges.

5...... Turn panel right side out; clip corners. Press upper and inner edges. Press up and stitch double-fold hem at lower edge, folding both curtain fabric and lining as one and using blindstitch or straight stitch. Press and stitch double-fold side hem on outer edge of curtain, folding both outer fabric and lining as one. Continue as on pages 83 and 84, steps 4 to 6.

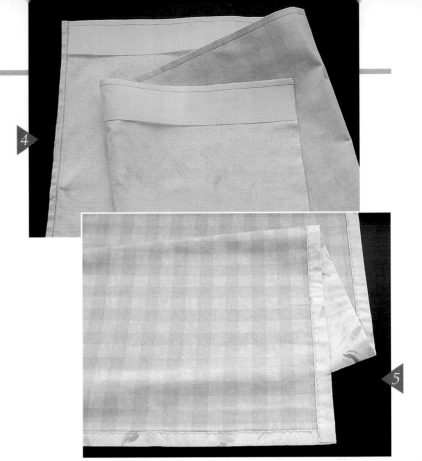

HOW TO SEW A *L*INED CURTAIN PANEL WITH AN ATTACHED FLOUNCE

1...... Follow steps 1 and 2, opposite; in step 2, omit welting along inner edge of curtain and apply to upper edge, if desired. Pin curtain and lining right sides together, and stitch ½" (1.3 cm) from raw edges at top and both sides. Press seam allowances open; trim seam allowances and clip corners. Turn right side out; press. Press up and stitch double-fold hem at lower edge.

2...... Fold allowance for flounce to right side of curtain. Continue as on pages 83 and 84, steps 4 to 6. For a scalloped edging on flounce, mark stitching line with chalk under each ring. With heavy-duty thread and ½" (1.3 cm) stitch length, gather fabric along marked line; hand-stitch in place on underside of flounce. Repeat at each curtain ring.

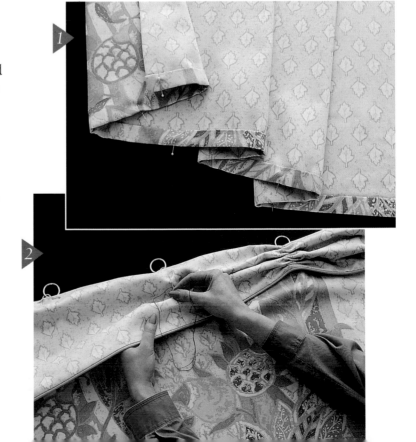

DOUBLE-LAYER SHEER PANELS

LIST *of* MATERIALS

▶ Decorator fabric in weight suitable for desired style.

▶ Decorator rod and sew-on rings, or cording or lacing.

CUTTING DIRECTIONS

For double-layer sheer panels, cut one panel from each fabric layer following the instructions for unlined panels on page 82, adding 1" (2.5 cm) to the upper edge instead of 7" (18 cm) and between 2" and 8" (5 and 20.5 cm) for desired double-fold hem at the lower edges, depending on desired finished hem depth, plus 12" to 20" (30.5 to 51 cm) for puddling on the floor, if desired.

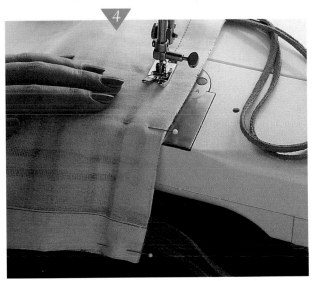

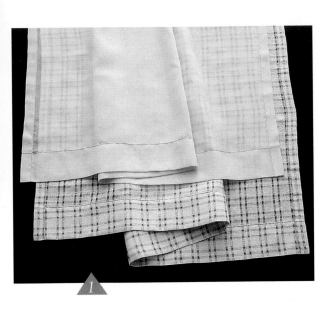

1 ...... Trim the panel for the underlayer of the curtain ½" (1.3 cm) shorter and ¾" (2 cm) narrower than the outer layer. Stitch desired double-fold hems at the lower edges of the panels, using blindstitch or straight stitch. Stitch 1" (2.5 cm) double-fold hems on the side edges of the panels.

2 ...... If embellishment, such as tassels or beads, is desired along the upper edge, follow steps 4 and 5 on pages 83 and 84, for curtain outer layer, but do not attach rings. If hanging curtain from tabs, pin or tape tabs plus any tassels or other embellishment at points that correspond to ring placement. Machine-baste in place.

3 ...... Pin right side of curtain outer layer to wrong side of curtain underlayer along upper edge, easing in fullness of outer layer; stitch 1" (2.5 cm) from upper edge; press seam allowance toward curtain. Fold along seamline, with right side of outer layer on top; press.

4 ...... Pin layers together along upper edge. Stitch 1" (2.5 cm) from upper edge through both layers. Attach decorative rings, if used. Continue as on page 84, step 6.

Banded
CURTAIN PANELS

For a striking tailored effect, make a curtain with contrasting banded edges. Combine two solid-colored fabrics to give a simple, yet dramatic, look. Or use a patterned fabric and a coordinating pattern or solid. Banding applied to the outer edges of a curtain panel can eliminate the need for side or lower hems. The instructions that follow are for a curtain banded on the side and lower edges. Mitered corners on the banding give it a finishing touch. This curtain is hung from rings on a decorative rod.

LIST *of* MATERIALS

► Decorator fabric, for the curtain.
► Coordinating decorator fabric, for the bands.
► Decorative rod and sew-on rings.

CUTTING DIRECTIONS

Determine the desired finished length of the panels. To determine the cut length, add ½" (1.3 cm) for the seam allowance at the lower edge, 4" (10 cm) for a 2" (5 cm) double-fold hem at the upper edge plus 12" to 20" (30.5 to 51 cm) for puddling on the floor, if desired. Decide on the desired fullness of the panels. Multiply the length of the rod, including side returns, if desired, times the desired fullness; divide this amount by the width of the fabric to determine the number of fabric widths required. Use full or half widths of fabric.

Cut two fabric strips for the side bands, with length equal to the length of the curtain along the side edges, and cut one fabric strip for the lower band, with length equal to the width of the curtain. The cut width of the band is 1" (2.5 cm) wider than the desired finished width of the band.

1...... Seam the fabric widths together. Finish seam allowances by serging or zigzagging. Press under ½" (1.3 cm) on one long edge of one side band. Pin band to curtain panel, with right side of band to wrong side of panel. Stitch a ½" (1.3 cm) seam, stopping ½" (1.3 cm) from lower edge. Repeat for band on opposite side.

2...... Press under ½" (1.3 cm) on one long edge of lower band. Pin to lower edge of curtain panel, with right side of band to wrong side of panel. Stitch ½" (1.3 cm) seam; start and stop ½" (1.3 cm) from side edges.

3...... Mark band for mitering, placing pins at inner corner as shown.

4...... Stitch miters, from pin marks at inner corner to end of stitching at outer corner; take care not to catch the curtain panel in stitching.

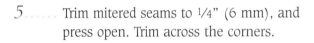
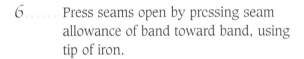

5..... Trim mitered seams to ¼" (6 mm), and press open. Trim across the corners.

6..... Press seams open by pressing seam allowance of band toward band, using tip of iron.

7..... Turn band to right side of curtain; press band, with the seamline on outer edge of curtain.

8..... Pin the band in place. Stitch around the band, close to the inner fold.

9..... At upper edge, stitch a 2" (5 cm) double-fold hem. Follow pages 83 and 84, steps 4 to 6.

Buttonhole CURTAIN PANELS

Simple in style, these no-fuss, unlined curtains have fresh appeal. The flat fabric panels slide onto the curtain rod through buttonholes, creating a curtain with soft, rolling curves.

LIST *of* MATERIALS

► Lightweight to mediumweight decorator fabric.

► Pole set or decorative curtain rod.

CUTTING DIRECTIONS

Determine the desired finished length of the panels by measuring from ¹/₂" (1.3 cm) above the top of the rod to the desired finished length of the curtain. Determine the necessary length of the buttonholes; the buttonhole length is equal to one-half the measurement around the rod plus ¹/₄" (6 mm).

The facing and turn-under at the top of the panel is equal to the length of the buttonholes plus 1¹/₂" (3.8 cm). The hem allowance at the bottom is equal to 6" (15 cm); this allows for a 3" (7.5 cm) double-fold hem. The cut length of each panel is equal to the desired finished length plus the facing and turn-under at the top plus the hem allowance at the bottom.

Determine the cut width of the fabric by multiplying the length of the rod times two; if you are sewing two curtain panels, divide this measurement by two to determine the cut width of each panel. For each panel, add 4" (10 cm) to allow for 1" (2.5 cm) double-fold side hems; if it is necessary to piece the fabric widths together, also add 1" (2.5 cm) for each seam.

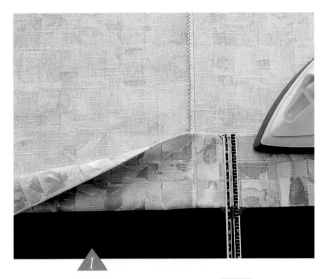

1 ...... Seam fabric widths, if necessary, for each curtain panel. Trim seam allowances to 1/4" (6 mm); finish, using zigzag or overlock stitch, and press to one side. At lower edge, press under 3" (7.5 cm) twice to wrong side; stitch close to inner fold.

2 ...... Press under 1/2" (1.3 cm) on the upper edge. Then press under an amount equal to buttonhole length plus 1" (2.5 cm). Stitch close to inner fold.

3 ...... Press under 1" (2.5 cm) twice on the sides; stitch close to the inner fold. Pin-mark placement for even number of buttonholes on top panel, centered on faced area; space end buttonholes 2" (5 cm) from sides, and remaining buttonholes 4" to 5" (10 to 12.5 cm) apart.

4 ...... Stitch vertical buttonholes. Weave panels onto pole or rod. Hang curtains.

Shaped
EDGES

To add style to a basic curtain, you can shape the edges along the top, sides, or bottom. Instead of turning up a hem allowance, finish off these shaped edges with facings. The facing can be made from self-fabric or contrasting fabric. If a print fabric is selected, check to see that light from the window will not cause the facing to shadow through to the right side of the curtain.

A contrasting facing applied to the front of a curtain instead of to the back side creates an interesting contrasting shaped band along the faced edge of the curtain. The technique used for shaped edges on a curtain can also be applied to the lower edge of a flounce or valance attached to a curtain. In this case, the entire flounce is faced. For added interest, a coordinating fabric welting or decorative welting can be inserted into the shaped seam.

When shaping the upper edge of a curtain that will be hung from rings or tabs, plan the placement of the rings or tabs to correspond to the repeat of the shaped pattern. Also plan to place a ring or tab at each end of a curtain panel.

CUTTING DIRECTIONS

Select one of the curtain styles from this book; then cut the curtain panels as directed for that specific curtain, substituting a ½" (1.3 cm) seam allowance for the hem allowance on the shaped edges. Determine the desired shaping for the edge of the curtain. For a shaped upper or lower edge, cut facing strips with the length equal to the width of the curtain panel at the upper or lower edge, including seam or hem allowances at the ends and the width equal to the desired width of the facing plus ½" (1.3 cm) for the outer seam allowance plus at least 1¼" (3.2 cm) for turn-under along the inner edge of the facing. For shaped side edges, cut facing strips with the length equal to the length of the curtain panel along the sides minus the hem allowances, plus ½" (2.5 cm) at each end for the seam allowances. The cut width of the facing is equal to the desired width of the facing plus ½" (1.3 cm) for the outer seam allowance plus at least 1¼" (3.2 cm) for turn-under along the inner edge of the facing.

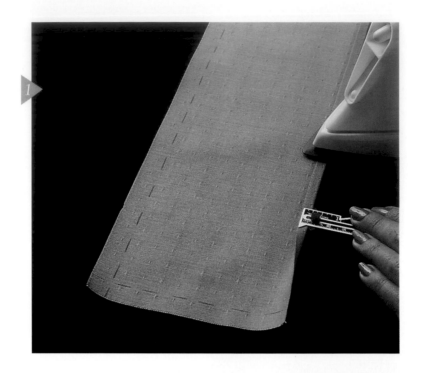

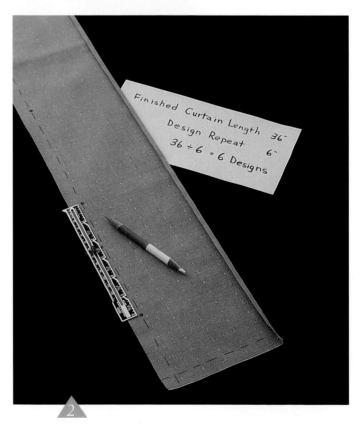

1 ...... Plan placement of any rings or tabs. Mark seamline on facing ½" (1.3 cm) from outer raw edge, using a marking pencil. Mark hemlines for curtain on each end of facing strip. Press up ¼" (6 mm) to wrong side on inner edge of facing.

2 ...... Measure distance between hemlines. Divide distance into an even number of sections equal to the width of the desired design repeat; mark repeat along marked seamline on the outer edge of the facing. If the upper edge of a curtain is to be shaped, the design repeat should match the placement of any rings or tabs used for hanging the curtain.

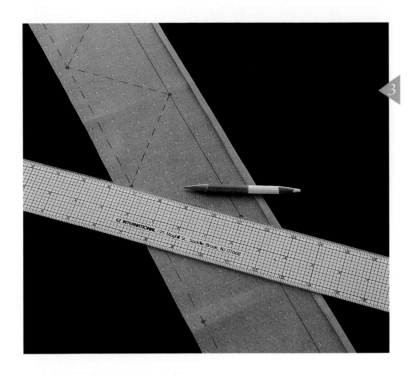

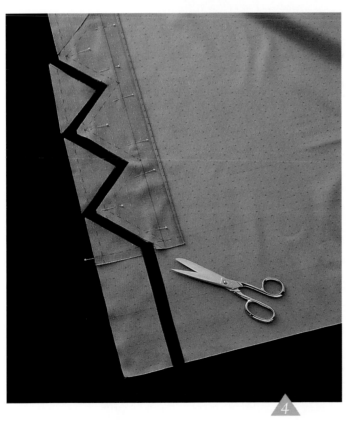

3 ..... Mark a line on facing, parallel to and a distance from outer seamline equal to the desired depth of shaped border. Mark points on second line equal to the width of pattern repeat. Draw desired shaped design between two marked points, using the marks on the outer seam allowance or depth line as guides. Repeat between remaining marked points.

4 ..... Add ½" (1.3 cm) seam allowances to shaped design. Place facing and curtain right sides together along raw edges. Pin facing to curtain panel. If shaping the upper edge of a curtain, fold double-fold hem allowance at each end. Cut shaped edge along marked cutting line. Make and attach welting to shaped edge as on pages 59 and 60, if desired.

continued

HOW TO SHAPE

5   Stitch shaped hem. Trim and clip seam allowances and hem allowances, if necessary; press. Reinforce any clipped points with small amount of fray preventer; allow to dry.

6   Turn facing right side out; press. Hem remaining edges. Pin facing to curtain along inner edge. Stitch close to folded edge. For a shaped upper edge, fold hem under diagonally at upper corner, if necessary, and hand-stitch, or for a shaped side edge, hand-stitch ends of facing in place. Complete curtain following the directions for the specific curtain chosen.

HOW TO MAKE A SHAPED EDGE ON A FLOUNCE

CUTTING DIRECTIONS

Cut the flounce as for curtain with a flounce on page 82; the cut width of the flounce is equal to the finished width of the curtain plus two ½" (1.3 cm) seam allowances. Cut the facing to the same size as the flounce.

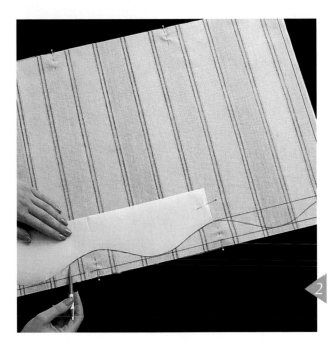

1...... Plan placement of rings as on pages 83 and 84, steps 4 and 5, for curtains hung with rings. Place facing and flounce right sides together, matching raw edges. Mark ½" (1.3 cm) seamlines for flounce on each end of facing strip, using a marking pencil. Mark seamline on lower edge of flounce facing, ½" (1.3 cm) from raw edge.

2...... Measure distance between side seamlines. Divide distance into an even number of sections equal to the width of the design repeat. Make a template of desired shape. Follow page 99, step 3, to mark the desired design along the lower edge of flounce, or make pattern the width of design repeat as shown. Continue as on pages 99 and 100, steps 4 to 6. Turn flounce right side out; press. Complete curtain with flounce as on page 87.

Unlined curtain panel with an attached flounce (page 84) is accented with a coordinating shaped band. Welting (page 59), inserted into the shaped seam, provides additional detail. The facing is applied to the right side of the curtain, instead of the back side, to create a contrasting border.

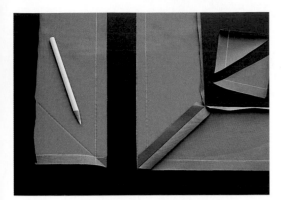

Follow page 98, step 1. With facing strips right sides together, fold back one corner until the short end is aligned with the line marked 1/2" (1.3 cm) from long edge; press. Unfold and mark line along crease line, using marking pencil. Pin facing strips right sides together; stitch along marked line, from outer raw edge to 1/4" (6 mm) from inner edge. Trim seam allowances 1/2" (1.3 cm) from stitching. Repeat for any remaining shaped sides. Continue as on pages 98 to 100, steps 2 to 6.

Unlined curtain panel (page 82) has scalloped edges along the inner side and lower edges. Miter corners as shown.

Unlined tab curtain (page 73) features a shaped upper edge.

Mark placement of tabs along upper edge of curtain; make scallop or other shaped design between tabs. Add 1/2" (1.3 cm) seam allowances to shaped edge. Make tabs as on page 75, step 2; fold in half, and baste in place along upper edge. Stitch 1/2" (1.3 cm) from shaped edge.

Tiebacks

Tiebacks are not only functional, they are often the focal point of a window treatment. For a stylish touch, they can be shaped in a gentle curve. Welting can be added to accent the edges of shaped tiebacks, perhaps repeating the detailing of a welted heading (page 61). Ruffled tiebacks work well on rod-pocket curtains. For a romantic look, make a 4" (10 cm) wide tieback with a large bow, or make a narrower tieback and tie it in a knot, as for the tabs on the tab curtains on page 78. Use fabric that matches the curtain for a subtle look, or choose a coordinating fabric for more impact.

Tiebacks are often positioned so they divide the curtain panel vertically into thirds. If the tiebacks are positioned one-third of the way from the bottom of the curtains, more window glass remains covered and the window appears wider. If they are positioned one-third of the way from the top, more window glass is revealed and the window appears longer. Also consider where to position the tieback in relation to any window details, such as sills or mullions.

Measure for the finished length of the tiebacks after the curtains are made and installed. Generally, the length of each tieback is one-half the total length of the curtain rod plus the projection of the rod. This allows each curtain panel to be pulled back to one-half its width. To visualize how the curtain will look tied back, wrap a cloth tape measure around the curtain panel at the desired tieback height and pull the panel back the desired distance. Angle the tape measure upward toward the outer edge of the curtain

where the tieback holder will be placed. For bow or knotted tiebacks, tie the tape measure and take into consideration the length desired for the tails on the bow or knot.

Shaped tiebacks (left) have a clean, tailored look. They may be sewn with or without welting.

Ruffled tiebacks add a romantic look to a window treatment.

Bow tieback (below) gives this curtain a soft touch.

LIST of MATERIALS

- ▶ Decorator fabric.
- ▶ Fusible polyester fleece or interfacing.
- ▶ Cording, for tiebacks with welting.
- ▶ Tieback rings, two for each tieback.
- ▶ Tieback holders, one for each tieback.
- ▶ Flexible curve or curved ruler.

CUTTING DIRECTIONS

Determine the desired finished length of the tiebacks (page 105). Make the pattern for the tiebacks as in steps 1 to 3, below. For each tieback, cut two pieces of decorator fabric and one piece of fusible fleece or interfacing, using the pattern.

If welting is desired, cut bias fabric strips to cover the welting, with the total length of the seamed strips 2" to 3" (5 to 7.5 cm) longer than the distance around the tieback. To determine the cut width of the strips, wrap a tape measure around the cording; the cut width of the strips is equal to the measurement around the cording plus 1" (2.5 cm).

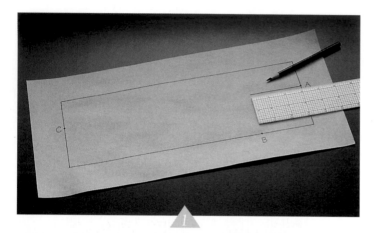

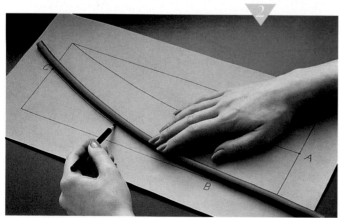

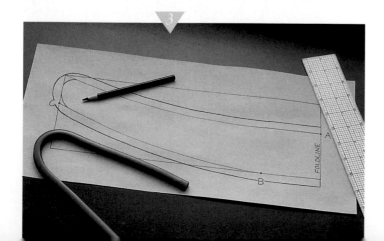

1 ...... Draw a rectangle on paper, with the short sides of the rectangle measuring 5" (12.5 cm); the long sides of the rectangle are equal to one-half the finished length of tieback. Mark Point A on one short side, 3" (7.5 cm) from the lower corner. Mark Point B on the long side, 3" (7.5 cm) from the same corner. Mark Point C on the opposite short side, 2" (5 cm) down from upper corner. Draw 3" (7.5 cm) line from Point A parallel to long sides.

2 ...... Use a flexible curve or a curved ruler to mark a gradual curve for the upper edge of the tieback, connecting the end of the 3" (7.5 cm) line to the upper corner on opposite side of the rectangle. For the lower edge of tieback, draw a curved line from Point C to Point B.

3 ...... Mark center foldline on side with Point A; round corners on the opposite side, for the return. Add ½" (1.3 cm) seam allowances at the upper and lower edges and around the return end.

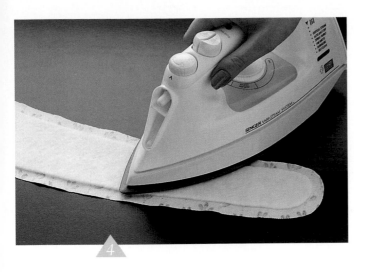

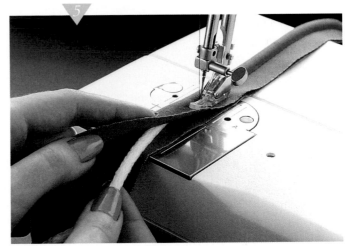

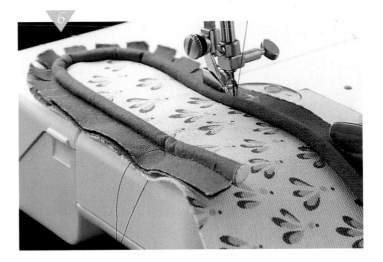

4...... Cut fabric and fusible fleece or interfacing, opposite. Trim ½" (1.3 cm) from the outer edge of fleece or interfacing; center on wrong side of outer tieback piece, and fuse in place. For tieback without welting, omit steps 5 to 9.

5...... Seam bias fabric strips together in ¼" (6 mm) seams. Fold fabric strip over cording, right side out, matching the raw edges. Using zipper foot, machine-baste close to the cording.

6...... Stitch the welting to the right side of tieback, matching raw edges; start 2" (5 cm) from the end of welting in an area of the tieback that will be concealed behind the curtain. To ease welting at the rounded corners, clip seam allowances to basting stitches.

7...... Stop stitching 2" (5 cm) from the point where the ends of the welting will meet. Cut off one end of welting so it overlaps the other end by 1" (2.5 cm).

continued

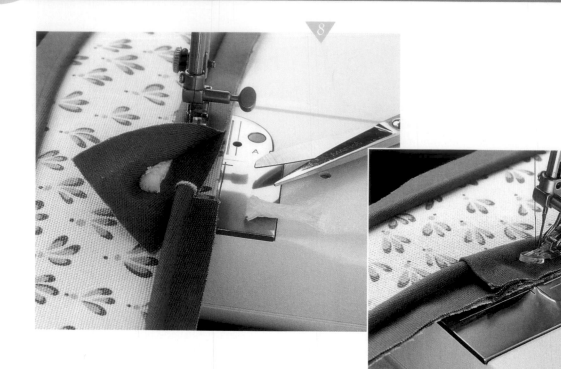

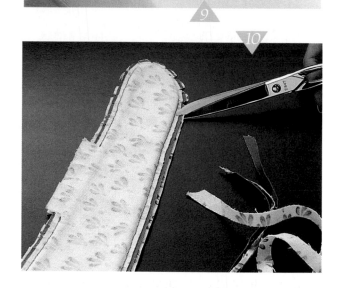

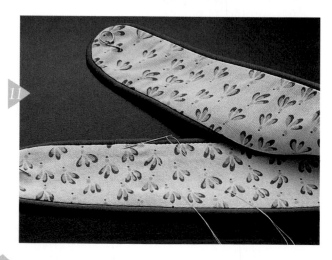

8...... Remove the stitching from one end of the welting, and trim the ends of the cording so they just meet.

9...... Fold under ½" (1.3 cm) of fabric on overlapping end. Lap it around the other end; finish stitching the welting to the tieback.

10.... Pin the outer tieback and lining pieces right sides together. Stitch ½" (1.3 cm) from raw edges, crowding cording; leave opening for turning. Trim seam allowances. Clip the curved upper and lower edges every ½" (1.3 cm); notch the curves of the return ends.

11.... Turn right side out; press. Slipstitch the opening closed. Secure tieback rings to wrong side of tieback, with one ring centered near each end. Attach the tieback to tieback holder (page 16).

LIST *of* MATERIALS

- ► Decorator fabric.
- ► Fusible interfacing.
- ► Tieback rings, two for each tieback.
- ► Tieback holders, one for each tieback.

CUTTING DIRECTIONS

Determine the desired finished length of the tiebacks (page 105). Cut one 3½" (9 cm) fabric strip for each tieback band, with the length of the strip equal to the finished length of the tieback plus 1" (2.5 cm); this gives a finished band width of 1¼" (3.2 cm). Cut a 2½" (6.5 cm) strip of fusible interfacing for each tieback, with the length equal to the finished length of the tieback.

For the ruffles, cut fabric strips on the crosswise grain, with the width of the strips equal to twice the desired finished width of the ruffle plus 1" (2.5 cm). The cut length of the strips is equal to two to two-and-one-half times the length to be ruffled.

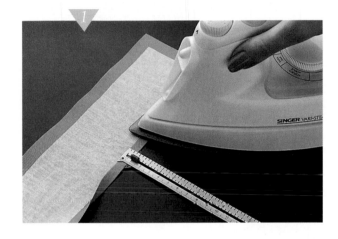

1...... Center the interfacing on wrong side of tieback; fuse in place. Press up ³⁄₈" (1 cm) on one long side of tieback.

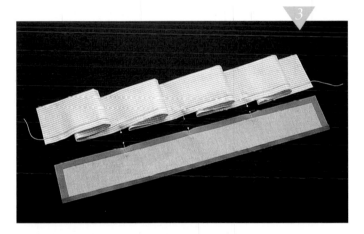

2...... Stitch the fabric strips for ruffle together in ¼" (6 mm) seams, right sides together; press open. Fold ends of strips in half lengthwise, right sides together; stitch across ends in ¼" (6 mm) seams. Turn right side out, and fold strip in half lengthwise, matching raw edges; press foldline and ends of ruffle strip.

3...... Zigzag over a cord on back side of ruffle strip within ½" (1.3 cm) seam allowance, stitching through both layers of ruffle strip. Divide ruffle strip and tieback band into fourths; pin-mark.

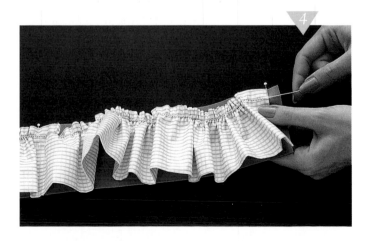

4...... Pin the ruffle strip to the unfolded side of the tieback band, right sides together, matching pin marks and raw edges, with ends of ruffle strip ½" (1.3 cm) from ends of the band. Pull up gathering cord on the ruffle to fit band; pin in place. Stitch ½" (1.3 cm) from raw edges.

continued

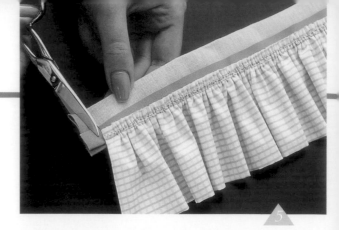
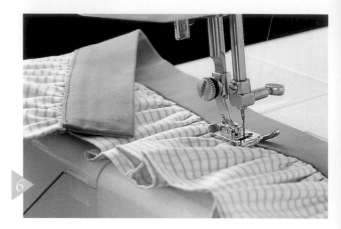

5...... Trim seam allowance of the ruffle to ¼" (6 mm). Fold the end of the band in half, wrong sides together, with the folded edge extending ⅛" (3 mm) beyond stitching line. Stitch ½" (1.3 cm) from end, taking care not to catch the ruffle in stitching; trim seam allowances. Repeat for the opposite end.

6...... Turn the band right side out, and press; the folded edge extends ⅛" (3 mm) below the stitching line on the back of the band. Pin in place; stitch in the ditch from the right side, catching the folded edge on the back of band. Secure tieback rings as in step 3, opposite; attach the tieback to the tieback holder (page 16).

HOW TO SEW *B*OW & KNOTTED TIEBACKS

LIST *of* MATERIALS

▶ Mediumweight to lightweight fabrics, appropriate for tie, that match or contrast with the curtain fabric. Allow extra fabric length for cutting on the bias.

▶ Sew-on or pin-on tieback rings.
▶ ¾" (2 cm) wood dowel, used for pressing.

CUTTING DIRECTIONS

For each tieback, cut a fabric strip on the bias, 1" (2.5 cm) longer than the desired finished length as determined on page 105, with the width of the fabric strip equal to twice the desired finished width plus 1" (2.5 cm).

1...... Fold the tieback in half, right sides together. Stitch ½" (1.3 cm) lengthwise seam, leaving opening for turning. Place ¾" (2 cm) dowel under seam, and press seam open.

2 ...... Center seam on back of tieback.
Trim ends of tiebacks diagonally,
if desired. Stitch ½" (1.3 cm)
seams at the ends; trim seam
allowances, and clip corners. Turn
the tieback right side out, and
press. Slipstitch the opening closed.

3 ...... Position tieback around curtain
and tie bow (a) or knot (b). Mark
location for tieback rings. Attach
pin-on tieback rings as shown (a).
Or remove tieback and stitch sew-
on tieback rings in place (b).

INDEX

COWLES Creative Publishing

President: Iain Macfarlane
Group Director, Book Development:
 Zoe Graul
Creative Director: Lisa Rosenthal
Senior Managing Editor:
 Elaine Perry

Creative Textiles™
CURTAINS
Created by: The Editors of Cowles
Creative Publishing

Project Manager: Amy Friebe

Art Director: Mark Jacobson

Editors: Dawn Anderson,
Linda Neubauer

Copy Editor: Janice Cauley

Desktop Publishing Specialist:
Laurie Kristensen

Project & Prop Stylist:
Coralie Sathre

Sample Manager:
Denise Bornhausen

Lead Samplemaker: Carol Pilot

Samplemakers: Arlene Dohrman,
Phyllis Galbraith, Virginia Mateen,
Michelle Skudlarek, Nancy Sundeen

Technical Photo Stylists:
Bridget Haugh, Nancy Sundeen

Studio Services Manager:
Marcia Chambers

Staff Photographers: Rex Irmen,
Chuck Nields, Gregory Wallace

Publishing Production Manager:
Kim Gerber

Printed on American paper by:
 Quebecor Printing
00 99 98 97 / 5 4 3 2 1

Cowles Creative Publishing, Inc. offers
a variety of how-to books. For infor-
mation write:
 Cowles Creative Publishing
 Subscriber Books
 5900 Green Oak Drive
 Minnetonka, MN 55343

LET *Curtains* EXPRESS YOUR FASHION FLAIR

Enrich the character of your home with curtains!

Bring softness and textural interest into every room with graceful curtains you sew yourself. Select fabrics and curtain styles that suit your personality and dress your windows with artistic taste.

Now you can:
▶ *Make curtains in fabrics that flatter your home's decor.*
▶ *Install window treatment hardware with confidence.*
▶ *Achieve high-style looks affordably.*

Beautiful photographs stimulate your creative talents and guide you through the entire curtain-making process.

ISBN 0-86573-412-7

EAN
9 780865 734128
90000

UPC
0 52944 01103 1

COWLES
Creative Publishing